SELECTED POEMS

1938–1988

Thomas McGrath

SELECTED POEMS

✦ 1938–1988 ✦

Edited and with an Introduction by
SAM HAMILL

COPPER CANYON PRESS

Poems in the first three sections are selected from the three previous volumes: *Movie at the End of the World* (Swallow Press, 1972); *Passages Toward the Dark* (Copper Canyon Press, 1982); and *Echoes Inside the Labyrinth* (Thunder's Mouth Press, 1983).

Some of the poems, or previous versions, from the fourth section appeared in the following magazines: *Caliban, Exquisite Corpse, Hurricane Alice, Masses & Mainstream, New Orleans Poetry Review, New York Quarterly, North Dakota Quarterly, Poetry East, The Subversive Agent,* and *TriQuarterly*.

The author acknowledges the support of the National Endowment for the Arts during the time some of this work was completed. Thanks also to Julie Hessler for her work on the manuscript.

ISBN : 1-55659-011-3 (cloth)
ISBN : 1-55659-012-1 (paper)
LIBRARY OF CONGRESS CATALOG CARD NUMBER : 87-72648

The publication of this book was supported by a grant from
the National Endowment for the Arts.

Copper Canyon Press is in residence with Centrum at Fort Worden State Park.

COPPER CANYON PRESS
Post Office Box 271, Port Townsend, WA 98368

✦ CONTENTS ✦

from PASSAGES TOWARD THE DARK

from ECHOES INSIDE THE LABYRINTH

NEW POEMS

TO MY SON TOM;

AND TO MARTIN, JOE, AND KATHLEEN

by Sam Hamill

> *"Poetry that will last a thousand generations
> comes only as an unappreciated life is passed."*
> — TU FU

The poetry and career of the T'ang poet, Tu Fu (712–770 AD), are marked by several major events: 1) the An Lu-shan Rebellion in the 750s; 2) poverty so severe that his own young son died of starvation; 3) years of wandering in exile in the north country, writing without an audience (his poems were "forgotten" for nearly three hundred years). Tu Fu honored a commitment to and belief in poetry unmatched by any writer of his time. Kenneth Rexroth has called Tu Fu "the greatest non-epic, non-dramatic poet who ever lived."

Certainly exile, poverty, and anonymity are often the earmarks of a poet's life. We remember that Dante was a prominent member of the city council in Florence from 1295 until his own exile in 1302; he served immediately after a time of crisis, the struggle for power between the "magnates" or wealthy and powerful, and the "popolo" or workingclass traders and shopkeepers. As the Guelfs, the wealthy merchant-class of Florence, regained power, Dante wrote *Le dolci rime d'amor* denouncing the "long-standing possession of wealth combined with pleasing manners," objecting strongly to the inherent hypocrisy. He also spoke out against the absolute power of the Pope, and, in late 1301, went into exile; in March, 1302, he was sentenced, in absentia, to death. He would never return to Florence. About this time, he wrote his great lyric, *Tre Donne* ("Three Ladies"), in which he says, referring to those in power, *"ma far mi poterian di pace dono./Pero nol fan che non san quel che sono."* ["They could make me a gift of peace. But because they do not understand me, they don't."] And Dante sees the three women, grandmother, mother, and daughter, as the embodiment of three kinds of Justice: divine, human, and written Law. When Dante makes Love acknowledge such a hierarchy, he presents us with a Justice that becomes attainable through its metaphysics, a Love that is no longer divorced from Justice.

Two examples illustrate the consequences of the search for Justice through poetry; two examples, one from the East and one from the West, frame a few remarks regarding the poetry (there is no "career") and achievement of Thomas McGrath who, in our time, exemplifies both the poet's struggle for Justice through Love, and the importance of commitment and responsibility.

In his earliest full-length book (*First Manifesto* was more a chapbook than a full-blown volume of poetry, and *The Dialectics of Love* was but a third of Alan Swallow's *Three Young Poets*), *To Walk a Crooked Mile* (Swallow, 1947), McGrath opens with "The Seekers," a poem written in Pueblo, Colorado, in 1940. Although a decidedly "new World" poem ("Our grandfathers were strangers . . ."), its thrust, especially in the closing stanza, expresses ideas the classical Chinese poet would readily embrace:

> "Every direction has its attendant devil,
> And their safaris weren't conducted on the bosses' time,
> For what they were hunting is certainly never tame
> And, for the poor, is usually illegal.
> Maybe with maps made going would be faster,
> But the maps made for tourists in their private cars
> Have no names for brotherhood or justice, and in any case
> We'll have to walk because we're going farther."

The poem was written a year after McGrath's graduation from the University of North Dakota, a year which would, under normal conditions, have been spent enjoying his Rhodes Scholarship. But he would not visit Oxford until the end of World War II. This war has been to McGrath as the An Lu-shan Rebellion was to Tu Fu: it signalled not only a world in chaos, but a loss of innocence and the lifelong struggle to cling to hope. World War II not only culminated in the invention of the Atomic Bomb, but simultaneously the end of a three-decade struggle for unionization and social organization for the oppressed, and the birth of the Cold War and all its attendant reactionary *realpolitik*. The war against Nazism was father and midwife to the Cold War. Every direction had its attendant devil.

And for the poor, for whom Justice has always been illegal, for the

poor whose sons are cannon fodder and whose dreams "are never fancy"?
Tu Fu said, "I am happiest among the best people I have found anywhere –
poor woodcutters and fishermen." Like Tu Fu, McGrath cannot, by virtue
of his erudition, be Common Man, but chooses to be among the common
people, to serve as advocate and, when necessary, agent provocateur. In
this, he resembles the Bodhisattvas – those who have become "enlight-
ened" but who refuse to enter Nirvana until such time as all sentient
beings become enlightened.

"Maybe," McGrath says, "with maps made going would be faster."
But there is no map for Justice. The maps are made "for tourists" rather
than for those for whom the going itself is everything. We go on foot be-
cause "we are going farther," that is, we are going into the realm of ideas,
we are entering pure process, the Tao. For McGrath, as for Tu Fu, the
means is the end, and the end is a beginning.

It is also useful to note the vast difference in McGrath's use of irony
from that of most scholar-poets. McGrath grounds the severe irony of the
last line in an idea that is both accessible and useful – it points the way
toward a fully-conscious awareness of being. It addresses Dante's notion
(and Tu Fu's) of metaphysical "justice" found within one's self. "If thee
does not turn to the inner light, where will thee turn?" Asked once about
the use and appropriateness of irony, Charles Olson declared, "I don't get
the 'iron' in it." Then he sat down and wrote, "I have had to learn the
simplest things / last. Which made for difficulties." McGrath begins with
a very complex simplicity, one which indeed rimes with that of Tu Fu.
Rather than searching his intellect for an ironic closure made entirely of
artifice, McGrath seeks limpidity which permits the truth of the poem to
find its own resonance – a purely organic irony pointing the way toward
the unending journey of the spirit.

Several poems later in the same book, there is a poem called "The
Tourists." I shall quote only from its repeated refrain:

> "Get off the highway, Brother, they are the tourists,
> Marveling sweetly along. . . .
> The place they seek, Brother, they cannot remember,
> Marveling sweetly along. . . .
> They cannot stop, Brother. Their hearts are too empty,
> Marveling sweetly along. . . .
> It is himself, Brother, that each one is looking for,
> Marveling sweetly along. . . .

Be careful, Brother, that you are not one of them,
Marveling sweetly along."

The poet sends a warning about the "dead faces" and "crazy eyes" of the passing populace with its "forlorn" voice. He says they will not stop "for love or for labor, for right or for wrong."

Tu Fu has a poem with a similar warning, albeit quite different circumstances. Visiting the site of the former Ts'ui family estate, he remembers the poet/painter Wang Wei, who accepted a government position only to find the consequences devastating to the family.

AT THE THATCHED HALL OF THE TS'UI FAMILY

It is autumn at the grass hut on Jade Peak.
The air is cool and clear.

Temple bells and chimes echo from the canyons.
Fishermen and woodsmen wind over sunset trails.

We fill our plates with chestnuts gathered in the valley
and rice grown in the village.

For what, Wang Wei?
Bamboo and pine, silent, locked behind a gate.

Just as McGrath, addressing his everyman as "brother," with all its confidentiality of diction, warns against infatuation with superficial travel, Tu Fu recalls the Buddhist/Taoist, Wang Wei, in his home village with its noble working class and implications represented by temple bells and windchimes and cool, clear air. There is calm in the village, and great dignity. There is plenty to eat. Still, Wang Wei wanted power. His government position forced him to leave behind the very source, according to Tu Fu, of his humility, of his greatness. For Tu Fu, as for McGrath, the common workaday experience is the true source of spiritual awakening, the source of the very concept of Justice.

Later, in *To Walk a Crooked Mile*, we come across a "Postcard" from Amchitka in the Aleutians where McGrath spent two years during the war. Remembering the midwestern summers and girls, he contrasts those images with the very real images of military movement, the "Nameless figures" which move "over the clamor / The yammer of trucks, in the dark, . . ." The poem reminds a reader of Chinese of Tu Fu's best-known anti-war poem, "Song of the War Wagons," with its opening image of clanging wagons and crying horses in the dust.

Next in McGrath comes a poem, "Emblems of Exile," which is so sturdy, so compassionate, and so truly felt that Tu Fu might have written it. This poem was somehow overlooked during the compilation of McGrath's 1972 collected poems, and so is missing from *The Movie at the End of the World.*

McGrath opens the first stanza with the image of a hunchback "with a halo of pigeons / Expelled from towers by the bells of noon / . . ." and, in the second stanza, to "the beggar in the empty street / On whom the hysteria of midnight falls . . ." This "prince of loneliness" calls "the hours of conscience" until, in the morning, the "supplicants" bribe him into silence. Calling them "symbols of bereavement," the poet intimates a death much larger than that of a more customary bereavement, and closes his poem with

"And if I assume the beggar's or the hunchback's shape
It is that I lack your grace which blessed my heart
Before the war, before the long exile
Which the beggarman mind accepts but cannot reconcile."

The mind of the poor, of the oppressed, accepts the conditions of exile, but the heart is incapable of reconciling either the injustice of the situation or the absurd logic which creates that situation in the first place. The pointed difference between acceptance of a situation and reconciliation with outrageous social conditions is one of the most recurrent themes in all of Chinese poetry.

AFTER THE HARVEST

The rice is cut and clouds glisten in the fields.
Facing Stone Gate, the river is low.

Winds shriek, ripping leaves from shrubs and trees.
At dawn, the pigs and chickens scatter.

Out of the distance, I hear the first sounds of battle.
The woodcutter's song is over. Soon he will leave the village.

Homeless and old, I long for a word from the homeland.
A wanderer, I place my trust in the world.

— Tu Fu

Like Tu Fu, McGrath has spoken often of the (to use Tu Fu's term) "essential goodness" of the poor and the oppressed. Besides the themes I have provided above (and the parallels between the two poets, the shared themes and attitudes, are all but inexhaustible) there are stylistic similarities in abundance. McGrath has written some of the most accomplished formal verses of mid-century, just as Tu Fu revitalized forms during his own time; McGrath and Tu share a common interest in inventing forms and exploring the organic line; each is very much concerned with sound and rhythm and harmony; each writes long poems, short poems, lyrics, polemics, homages, praises, and invective (although Tu Fu wrote very little of the latter). Tu Fu writes praises for flowers, rice, or wine; McGrath writes praises for bread or for beer. McGrath's *Open Songs* and *Letters to Tomasito* are perfect counterparts to Tu Fu's short Taoist poems (or, for that matter, to the *haiku's* predecessor, the *tanka* in Japanese). And McGrath writes new lyrics to an old song (as he did for Cisco Houston to the tune "Matty Grove") just as the *tz'u* poets of the T'ang and Sung wrote new lyrics for their old tunes.

Nearly all poets attempt, at one time or another, to write an *ars poetica*. Most often, the result is self-inflation and/or leaden seriousness. But both McGrath and Tu Fu find enormous good humor in the situation of the poet. McGrath begins his "You Can Start the Poetry Now, Or: News from Crazy Horse" with a drunken poet on stage, probably in some tavern, mumbling into a microphone, "– I guess all I'm trying to say is I saw Crazy Horse die for a split level swimming pool in a tree-house owned by a Pawnee–Warner Brothers psychiatrist about three hundred feet above –" when someone in the audience, not knowing whether this unrhymed diatribe is the poem or the introduction to a poem, calls out, first softly, "You can start the poetry now." But the poet continues to mumble along, and the demand to "start the poetry now" grows louder and louder. It is a beautifully funny assessment of a bad poetry reading, and it teaches the young poet a great deal without harangues or insults to poetry itself; it also says a lot about those who have never learned how to listen to a public reading.

And another well-known poem is McGrath's, "Ars Poetica: Or: Who Lives in the Ivory Tower?" with its references to roundelays and sestinas, Hedy Lamarr, Gable, Louella Parsons, and the "to hell with the Bard of Avalon and to hell with Eliot Auden." And of course, the poem's famous closing line: "Your feet are muddy, you son-of-a-bitch, get out of our ivory tower."

Tu Fu approaches the poem about writing from another equally humorous and practical angle, by addressing the necessary arguments of like-minded poets in his "To Li Po on a Spring Day" –

There's no one quite like you, Li Po,
you live in my imagination.

You sing as sweet as Yui,
and still retain Pao's nobility.

Under spring skies north of Wei,
you wander into the sunset

toward the village of Chiang-tung.
Tell me, will we ever again

buy another keg of wine
and argue over prosody and rhyme?

Tu is less ironic in his references to past masters, preferring to hold them up as standards which he finds Li Po has met. But the spirit of the poem finds a counterpart in McGrath's drunken mumbler who, no doubt, is as earnest as any poet. And while Tu makes clear that what he really misses is the drinking and arguing – traditional camaraderie among poets of all tongues – he manages to draw a smile from the reader while simultaneously revivifying the need for a dialectic. Tu's homage to Li Po might also recall McGrath's wonderful satire, "Driving Toward Boston I Run Across One of Robert Bly's Old Poems." McGrath, like Tu Fu, joins criticism to humor, caustic argument with good cheer.

But neither is a poet whom Plato would admit into the Republic. Plato has Socrates tell Glaucon, "We must remain firm in our conviction that hymns to the gods and praises of famous men are the only poetry which ought to be admitted into our State. For if you go beyond this and allow the honeyed muse to enter, either in epic or lyric verse, not law and the reason of mankind, which by common consent have ever been deemed best, but pleasure and pain will become the rulers in our State. . . ." Socrates goes on to warn Glaucon about the "mob of sages circumventing Zeus," and the "subtle thinkers" who quarrel with philosophy and who are, after all, "mere beggars" in the State. Plato, embarrassed by the emotional truth of the poet who is "drawling out his sorrows in long oration, or weeping, or smiting his breast," admits only the singer of praises for famous men and gods, in short, the platitudinizers of the powerful, into his State. And Plato speaks for every State.

For Tu Fu, the result was a decade and more of wandering through Shensi, Kansu, and Szechuan – the Chinese equivalent of the Badlands – a beggar in a feudal time. He had criticized the ruling class. He had been an advocate, a voice of compassion, a deeply religious poet with no formal religion. He fought a daily war with bitterness, only to write some of the most humane poetry in all history.

Five-hundred-odd years later, Dante, writing in exile, would proclaim, "Let the eyes that weep and the mouths that wail be those of mankind whom it concerns." And still later, in the *Convivio*, states, "I have gone through nearly all the regions to which the tongue [Italian] reaches, a wanderer, a beggar showing against my will the wounds which fortune makes, and which are often unjustly held against the one who bears those wounds. . . . I have appeared to the eyes of many who had perhaps imagined me, through fame, to be otherwise." And, in exile, Dante wrote that masterpiece of precision, thirty-three cantos each, of Hell, Purgatory, and Paradise. In Dante, love and justice become inseparable. We remember, if only by reputation, that Dante survived his Hell and entered Paradise; but we should not forget that Paradise lasts but a day, and Hell is at least seven times longer.

And six-hundred-odd years after that, Thomas McGrath finds himself on the West Coast of North America, in the mid-century, where "things are happening," and the Army-McCarthy Hearings have ended, his old friends can't get themselves into print, Dalton Trumbo and many others are growing famous on the Blacklist, and Eisenhower is giving speeches warning about the "Military-Industrial Complex," and some black folk down South are talking civil rights. The McCarthy House Subcommittee on Un-American Activities came along when McGrath was in his late twenties and early thirties. It was a daily reality seeing newspaper headlines and photographs of McCarthy, Richard Nixon, and Robert Kennedy as they accused, tried, and sentenced people from all walks of life on the basis of testimony which was itself based upon lies, innuendo, and public fear. It was disillusioning in the same way World War I served to shake the bearings of an older generation.

McGrath sits down one day and writes:

"– 'From here it is necessary to ship all bodies east.' "

It is a line he had carried around for years without finding a way to begin what he hoped would be a poem long enough to invest several years in writing. This time, he wrote it down. And then he wrote:

"I am in Los Angeles, at 2714 Marsh Street,
Writing, rolling east with the earth, drifting toward Scorpio,
Hoping toward laughter and indifference."

The rest we know, or ought to know, in the name of poetry and justice. McGrath invests a quarter-century in his poem. He writes his Christmas poem all during the war in Viet Nam. He writes it while the Freedom Riders ride. He writes on through the funerals of the Kennedys and King. He writes while Nixon tells us lies.

And he continues to write little songs, formalist verses, neo-Nerudean polemics, drinking songs, Taoist poems, elegies, and praises – many of his best poems. And because, to quote William Irwin Thompson, "One instinctively suspects people who meet in drawing rooms to praise the peasant over tea and cakes," McGrath returns to the "cold, black North" where he was born, writing in a kind of self-imposed exile, in compassion- ate, passionate "laughter and indifference."

Poetry and exile – how very often they combine. One remembers Neruda in the Orient, innumerable Chinese sages, the Modernists, the Romantics, Tu Fu, Dante, and McGrath; one recalls Rilke's homelessness, Rexroth's self-exile in Santa Barbara and his teaching for what amounted almost to Teaching Assistant-ship wages at "Surf Board Tech" (University of California, Santa Barbara), the exile of Ritsos and Seferis, and the mur- der of García Lorca when he refused to leave Spain. One becomes resigned to the circumstances without accepting the injustice; the struggle with the self is greater than the struggle with the State. No poet wants to inhabit Plato's Republic; but neither does one wish for the life of exile and/or poverty. To write is to speak. To speak implies the necessity of audience.

Several years ago, McGrath was questioned by a student about "the writing program" at Moorhead – what would be expected, and what a graduate of the program might look forward to. "The first thing I tell my students," McGrath replied, "is that most of my former students drive right down the road and get a job in the beet-packing plant." His remark says as much about what a poet's responsibilities are as it does about the general situation of poetry in our country. Such is the justice of poetry . . . for McGrath, for Dante, for Tu Fu. . . .

It might have been different. I doubt McGrath ever courted the New York publishing scene. It certainly never courted him. But if it were oth- erwise, it wouldn't be McGrath. As with Tu Fu, his end lies in his means. The truth of the poem is in the voice, not printed on the paper a "pub- lisher" buys and sells. Poetry contains silence, but is not silent. Nor is Justice. Nor, often, love.

Praise for the achievement of Thomas McGrath is long overdue. And it is only now beginning. But, lest we run headstrong through these paral- lels with Dante and with Tu Fu, let me close by quoting a quatrain from

Senzaki, one which would, I'm sure, please Tu Fu and Dante both, one which serves as epigraph to one of the greatest long poems of our century:

> In the moonlight,
> The shadow of the bamboo
> Is sweeping the great stairs;
> But the dust is not stirred.

Because it is so completely readable and so much of-a-piece, McGrath's great *Letter to an Imaginary Friend* (*Parts I & II* from Swallow Press, 1970; *Parts Three & Four* from Copper Canyon Press, 1985) has not been excerpted or condensed for this *Selected Poems*; otherwise, this volume spans McGrath's *oeuvre*: over fifty years of poetry. Presented here in roughly chronological order, these poems represent a lifetime's struggle to achieve clarity of vision and to reveal a living soul without masks, without apology or self-pity, a poet for whom meaning and music are one – in the saying of the poem, the poem, for a moment, is.

Contrary to the beliefs of traditionalists and free versifiers alike, the lyric is the most difficult poetry to write. Any flaw in the rhythm or tone, any false note or forced emotion results in an audible warp – hearing the false note, the listener loses a few words, captivated not by the poem itself, but by the flaw.

McGrath writes some of the finest cadenced poetry of the twentieth century. At his best, he is metrically irregular, the lines lifting and falling with vowel and consonant reverberating through the rhythms of a carefully speaking voice. He also composes in a quantitative line, writes parodies (see "Driving Toward Boston I Run Across One of Robert Bly's Old Poems"), variations of haiku, and perfect little Imagist poems. Now Orphic, now extremely personal, there is almost no subject unsuitable for a McGrath poem. His virtuosity is staggering. Some of the poems are, as Kenneth Rexroth said of Lawrence's, "nobly disheveled"; some are semiprecious stones; a few are jewels.

It was not my intention to compile a "greatest hits." With the very generous assistance of Jay White and with the participation and cooperation of the poet, we came to an agreement on what should stand as the representative selection of fifty years of writing. Most of the best-known poems are included; also included are poems we felt most deserving of another reading, as in "The Little Odyssey of Jason Quint, of Science, Doctor."

Throughout these poems, everywhere evident, is Thomas McGrath's great good humor, an astonished observer awed by beauty and sadness and *joie de vivre* – camaraderie found only in the hope for justice and in his fierce commitment to compassion and common good.

from

◆ THE MOVIE ◆

AT THE END OF THE WORLD

◆ GET OUT OF TOWN

Get out of town before it's too late
While the speedboat is frozen in the arctic lake
While the cops are snoring in the frost-hung parlor
And the shotgun hidden under crumpled pillows.

Get out of town, cross the winter mountain.
There are arteries hardening. The mob yells murder,
But be stayed no one, yourself no traitor –
They will not be saved, themselves not try to.

Get out of town while the going is good.
Say the hard word. Kiss the girls goodby.
Let the boys wait forever in the gloomy barrens
A thousand miles from water and as far from wood.

✦ UP THE DARK VALLEY

After the lean road looping the narrow river,
At a break in the valley, turned northward up the coulee,
Past the slow shallows where minnows, a tin flash
Patterned the trellised shadow. Then, leaving behind the last trees,
The spider sun laid on the hot face a tight miraculous web.

Northward then. All afternoon beneath my feet the ground gave
Uneven going. The colorless silence, unraveled by the flies,
Stitched again by the locusts, was heard, was smelled –
Swamp-smell, dead coulee water.
                                          And the easy hills,
Burnt brown, green, grass color, went on through the afternoon,
Then blue-gray in the blue shadow. The path went on.
Darkness hid in the draws. I was soon surrounded.
Only the wind sound now. All through the evening,
Homeward I walk, hearing no human sound.

The birds of darkness sang back every call.

✦ WOODCUT

It is autumn but early. No crow cries from the dry woods.
The house droops like an eyelid over the leprous hill.
In the bald barnyard one horse, a collection of angles
Cuts at the flies with a spectral tail. A blind man's
Sentence, the road goes on. Lifts as the slope lifts it.

Comes now one who has been conquered
By all he sees. And asks what – would have what –
Poor fool, frail, this man, mistake, my hero?

More than the hands on the lines and the back aching,
The daily wrestle with the angel in the south forty,
More than this forever lonely round
Round hunger and impotence, the prickly pair:
Banker or broker can have dreamed no fate
More bankrupt than this godlike heresy
Which asks of love more leave than extended credit,
Needs comradeship more than a psalm or surely these
Worn acres even if over them
Those trained to it see signs of they say God.

✦ THE TOPOGRAPHY OF HISTORY

All cities are open in the hot season.
Northward or southward the summer gives out
Few telephone numbers but no one in our house sleeps.

Southward that river carries its flood
The dying winter, the spring's nostalgia:
Wisconsin's dead grass beached at Baton Rouge.
Carries the vegetable loves of the young blonde
Going for water by the dikes of Winnetka or Louisville,
Carries its obscure music and its strange humour,
Its own disturbing life, its peculiar ideas of movement.
Two thousand miles, moving from the secret north
It crowds the country apart: at last reaching
The lynch-dreaming, the demon-haunted, the murderous virgin South
Makes its own bargains and says change in its own fashion.
And where the Gulf choirs out its blue hosannas
Carries the drowned men's bones and its buried life:
It is an enormous bell, rung through the country's midnight.

*   *   *

Beyond the corrosive ironies of prairies,
Midnight savannas, open vowels of the flat country,
The moonstruck waters of the Kansas bays
Where the Dakotas bell and nuzzle at the north coast,
The nay-saying desolation where the mind is lost
In the mean acres and the wind comes down for a thousand miles
Smelling of the stars' high pastures, and speaking a strange language –
There is the direct action of mountains, a revolution,
A revelation in stone, the solid decrees of past history,
A soviet of language not yet cooled nor understood clearly:
The voices from underground, the granite vocables.
There shall that voice crying for justice be heard,
But the local colorist, broken on cliffs of laughter,
At the late dew point of pity collect only the irony of serene stars.

*   *   *

Here all questions are mooted. All battles joined.
          No one in our house sleeps.
And the Idealist hunting in the high latitudes of unreason,
By mummy rivers, on the open minds of curst lakes
Mirrors his permanent address; yet suffers from visions
Of spring break-up, the open river of history.
On this the Dreamer sweats in his sound-proof tower:
All towns are taken in the hot season.

How shall that Sentimentalist love the Mississippi?
His love is a trick of mirrors, his spit's abstraction,
Whose blood and guts are filing system for
A single index of the head or heart's statistics.
Living in one time, he shall have no history.
How shall he love change who lives in a static world?
His love is lost tomorrow between Memphis and
                the narrows of Vicksburg.

But kissed unconscious between Medicine Bow and Tombstone
He shall love at the precipice brink who would love these mountains.
Whom this land loves shall be a holy wanderer,
The eyes burned slick with distances between
Kennebunkport and Denver, minted of transcience.
For him shall that river run in circles and
The Tetons seismically skipping to their ancient compelling music
Send embassies of young sierras to nibble from his hand.
His leaves familiar with the constant wind,
Give, then, the soils and waters to command.
Latitudinal desires scatter his seed,
And in political climates sprout new freedom.
But curst is the water-wingless foreigner from Boston,
Stumping the country as others no better have done,
Frightened of earthquake, aware of the rising waters,
Calling out "O Love, Love," but finding none.

✦ THE DROWNED MAN:
DEATH BETWEEN TWO RIVERS

1.

Someone moves through the jungle
Where the East Side rears its neo-Tammany escarpment
Over East River toward the city of the dead, toward Brooklyn;
Past the opulent stinks, the sinks and pits of corruption,
Where canned heat dreams are pregnant with rancid dragons –
Immaculate conceptions! –

Someone, someone is moving:
The feet go eastward, past the callow pimps
Pasted on door-ways and past the wise, new-minted
Eyes of the semi-virgins. Waters of Israel
Open in paths before him: the Leaning Man,
Comes out of Egypt.

By the waters of his captivity,
He leans on the river rail. The enchanted liner,
A breathing bird upon the water's breast,
Beats for the windy capes, the secret cities
Of the lush South. The river stinks. Behind him,
The towers of Babylon –

Altar of profane love,
Each marvelous marble phallus. On the walls
The handwriting winks in easy translations of neon.
Over him the bridge no one has written an ode to,
And northward the monstrous Tri-borough, seeking direction
Puts out its feelers:

A symbol of indecision
For the Leaning Man, the semi-vertical man,
Man by a river, looking to westward, knowing
The terrible land wherein the Lost Tribes dwell,
And, hatches closed against night, the known world
Slowly submerging.

He assumes vertical stature
Standing, as the deck lists under the lip of water
He looks toward the city, inventing impossible justice:
Recalls other cries, and decision matures, remembering
Metal of headlines masked as life preservers:
Dives from the railing.

The East River upbore him:
Two-thirds submerged in the riptides under the bridgeheads,
In a montage of oil-smear, rotten fruit and wreckage –
Christ! his poor face split like a seed-pod sowing
In the crucified night an improbable human anguish –
The face of my brother!

2.

Full fathom five the East Side lies;
The West Side lies five fathom under.
A slow sea-change in the drowned veins,
The unfortunate human condition creates its pitiful wonders:
Unlikely fear has deepened into gills
And cynic's scales – armor against laughter;
The dearest nightmare is the dream of waking,
Waking to choke in the drowsy midnight waters:
The drowned eye builds in token its cheap ambiguous altars
In the Java Deeps of the Leaning Men, where the drunken small boat founders.

The little yachts of extended credit
Are lost where the naked rocks are lying
But the mighty slave-galleys of surplus value
Move on these human deeps, majestic, the black flag flying.
At dawn in Wall Street the gentle fishers
Dapple with nets the sunshot sound,
And all but the strangest swimmers are taken:

Between two rivers where my brother drowned –
In the waters of Manhattan, where he last went down,
Where the mad boy catches at his sunken moons and darkens the night
        with crying.

           *   *   *

I heard them crying halfway up Delancy –
Poverty halleluiahs, neither private nor fancy.
        Tell me, Stranger, who was lost,
        Father, son or wholly ghost?

3.

No one has seen in the leaves, in the dark, crowding,
The immaculate mutinous bodies, or, shyly, the brutal
Inhuman faces of angels. Only of birds,
In the empty dark, the shameless voices puzzling
Some last year's song. The news is bad. Angels
Are scarce this year. A ghost perhaps? But no one
No one walking on a windward water. No one.

Darkness over the waters. The tame tides
Set to the impersonal moon which over Brooklyn
Scatters its loose money. The East River
Constant, turns to the inconstant sea,
A cortege of tired cigars, old photographs,
Letters of credit with their mouths sewn shut, newspapers,
Paler than funeral flowers, its dead men's bones
(All abstract emblems of our civilization)
Bearing my brother:

The tides set toward the Jersey coast, push southward,
Slack from wreck-wreathed Hatteras. And where
The Gulf Stream washes toward the glittering North,
The mystic fog-hung latitudes of myth,

Do those bones live?
                              Or in the under sea
Processional of equatorial drift,
Or swept beyond Lands End, tossed in the wind,
Or in the mile-long funnels of the dreaming interior
Made part of the steaming legend-haunted sea?

                    *   *   *

Someone is dying, someone is being born:
Out of the salt blood, fiercer than the sea
Where the human tide makes in the evening rush:
Grand Central—Times Square undertow,
Setting to a black moon over Harlem:
Something is dying. Something is being born.

There are ghosts among us. Who was that
In the tombstone hat, the meek hick jacket?
Out of a deeper drowning than the sea,
Out of the cynic north, in that season, the second, where all illusion is lost,
The obscure, terrible coming of our holy ghost.

I did not recognize him under the bridge:
Saw only our human weakness as denominator in that fraction.
But later, I remembered in the flat-lands hearing
That mountain speech, and in the mountains hearing
His speech as of cities, and in the cities hearing
His silence of hawks. And it was easy then
To think how tides had shortened the tough Rockies,
Washed out the Kansas Coast or in the river haunted
Landscapes of New England bore with them this specter
Which haunts all countries in the fifth season.
                              And felt,
Ambiguous as hope but stronger, something crowding
The hollow channels of the blood, or swept between
The red islands, speaking with the timid tongue,

Naming the devils at the several compass points,
With words for the nightmares of our sunken world,
Calling insurrection, knocking at the tame heart –
"Sleeper awake."

*　*　*

The ambulance siren drifts in the blue night air.
With tentative provocation the first stars
Put out thin stalks of light, placing their formal
Decorations on a sleeping child. Somewhere
A nightmare sharpens and a man cries out. The young
Mother feels the child kick in her belly.
Once. Twice. And deeper than pain she feels
How out of the submerged life, the human winter,
The young god comes to whom all eyes shall turn.
One class dies. Another is being born.
Word becomes flesh. The Specter becomes real.

Someone is born with the bright face of your brother.

◆ THE SEEKERS

Pueblo, Colorado 1940

Our grandfathers were strangers and their absurd notions
Said uncle to a century that built few fences;
Pragmatists, with six-guns, their dreams were never fancy;
Beyond their mustaches, their eyes eloped with nations.
Their caravans set wagon tongues at a peculiar star;
Led at last to mountains, they sought to map Fidelity –
Went loco in windy canyons, but, lost, they looked
        harder and harder.

Our fathers, more complex and less heroic,
Were haunted by more ghosts than an empty house.
Their joy was to thumb their hearts over. Masked like Freud
They entered their unconscious by the second story.
But what they were seeking, or how it looked or sounded,
We heard about only once in a blue moon,
Though they expected to know it if they ever found it.

Every direction has its attendant devil,
And their safaris weren't conducted on the bosses' time,
For what they were hunting is certainly never tame
And, for the poor, is usually illegal.
Maybe with maps made going would be faster,
But the maps made for tourists in their private cars
Have no names for brotherhood or justice, and in any case
We'll have to walk because we're going farther.

✦ DEEP SOUTH

Baton Rouge, 1940

These are savannas bluer than your dreams
Where other loves are fashioned to older music,
And the romantic in his light boat
Puts out among flamingos and water moccasins
Looking for the river that went by last year.

Even the angels wear confederate uniforms;
And when the magnolia blooms and the honeysuckle,
Golden lovers, brighter than the moon,
Read Catullus in the flaring light
Of the burning Negro in the open eye of midnight.

And the Traveller, moving in the hot swamps,
Where every human sympathy sends up the temperature,
Comes of a sudden on the hidden glacier,
Whose motives are blonder than Hitler's choir boys.

Here is the ambiguous tenderness of 'gators
Trumpeting their loves along a hundred miles
Of rivers writhing under trees like myths –
And human existence pursues the last,
The simple and desperate life of the senses.
Since love survives only as ironic legend –
Response to situations no longer present –
Men lacking dignity are seized by pride,
Which is the easy upper-class infection.

The masters are at home in this merciless climate
But deep in the caves of their minds some animal memory
Warns of the fate of the mammoth at the end of the ice-age;
As sleeping children a toy, they hug the last, fatal error,
But their eyes are awake and their dreams shake as with palsy.

*   *   *

Over Birmingham where the blast furnace flowers
And beyond the piney woods in cotton country,
Continually puzzling the pale aristocrats,
The sun burns equally white man and black.

The labor which they do makes more and more
Their brotherhood condition for their whole existence;
They mint their own light, and their fusing fires
Will melt at last these centuries of ice.

This is a nightmare nimble in the Big House,
Where sleepers are wakeful, cuddling their terror,
In the empty acres of their rich beds, dreaming
Of bones in museums, where the black boys yawn.

✦ A LONG WAY OUTSIDE YELLOWSTONE

Cheyenne, Wyoming, 1940

Across the tracks in Cheyenne, behind the biggest billboard,
Are a couple of human beings who aren't in for the Rodeo.
A week out of Sacramento, Jack, who was once a choir boy,
And Judy, a jail-bird's daughter, make love against the cold.
He gets the night freight for Denver. She hitches out for Billings.
But now under one blanket they go about their business.
Suppose you go about yours. Their business is being human,
And because they travel naked they are fifty jumps ahead of you
And running with all their lights on while half the world is blacked out.

Poverty of all but spirit turns up love like aces
That weren't in the deck at all.
                                        Meanwhile the cold
Is scattered like petals of flowers down from the mountains of exile
And makes comradeship essential, though perhaps you choose not to believe it.
That doesn't matter at all, for their hands touching deny you,
Becoming, poor blinded beggars, pilgrims on the road to heaven.

Back in the Park, at the best hotel, it is true
The mountains are higher, and the food oftener, and love
As phony as a nine-dollar bill. Though perhaps
When the millionaire kisses the Princess farewell (he's going nowhere)
She weeps attractively in the expensive dark, moving –
O delicately – among the broken hearts, perhaps haunted,
Wondering if hers is among them. Or perhaps not.

✦ LOVE IN A BUS

Chicago, 1942

It was born in perhaps the Holland Tunnel,
And in New Jersey opened up its eyes,
Discovered its hands in Pennsylvania and
Later the night came.

The moon burned brighter than the dreams of lechers –
Still, they made love halfway to Pittsburgh,
Disturbing the passengers and sometimes themselves.
Her laughter gamboled in the bus like kittens:
He kissed with his cap on, maybe had no hair.
I kept remembering them even beyond Chicago
Where everyone discovered a personal direction.
She went to Omaha; he went south; and I,
Having nothing better, was thinking of chance –
Which has its mouth open in perpetual surprise –
And love. For even though she was a whore
And he a poor devil wearing built-up heels,
Still, love has light which like an early lamp
Or Hesperus, that star, to the simplest object
Lends a magnificent impersonal radiance,
Human, impermanent and permanently good.

◆ DEATH FOR THE DARK STRANGER

The knave of darkness, limber in the leaves
Where the blue water blues the green of willows
And the blue geese tamely admire the wild mallows
In that always summer where memory grieves and lives,
Was a childhood friend perhaps, but now has other loves.

Or he posed as an uncle, maybe, wise,
An old head among the winds of that region,
An impartial umpire while the wars were raging –
Or he was the enchanting stranger with Spartan ways
Whose judgments were always final. But whoever the Presence was

He was cop in your county – and nothing ever less –
(Though always, in your private legend, one you knew)
Saying "keep off the grass" and "no, no,"
Infecting all your hopes with sense of loss
And to all new settings-forth crying "alas, alas."

For he is the heart's head-keeper, the bland
Insane director of a rich asylum
Where sanity is poisoned. He is king on that island,
Society's hangman, super-ego, he was born blind;
His loves are like Hitler's: upperclass and blond.

He is the keeper of what we never had,
And in order to arrive where we have never been
He must be numbered with the enemy slain –
His voice be loud with those we never heed:
His death alone unites the warring heart and head.

And wakes the proud blood of those fierce birds –
Else bewitched by their image in the dead still water
Of that enchanted summer where their wild hearts wither
(As our will is weakened by a crutch of words) –
So again the miraculous thunder of discovering wings is heard.

✦ THE HEROES OF CHILDHOOD

The heroes of childhood were simple and austere,
And their pearl-handled six-guns never missed fire.
They filled all their straights, were lucky at dice,
In a town full of badmen they never lost face.
When they looked under beds there was nobody there.

We saluted the outlaw whose heart was pure
When he stuck up the stage or the mail car –
Big Bill Haywood or Two Gun Marx,
Who stood against the bankers and all their works –
They robbed the rich and gave to the poor.

But we in our time are not so sure:
When the posse catches us our guns hang fire,
And strung up from the wagon-tongues of long reflection
Our hearts are left hanging by the contradiction
Which history imposes on our actions here.

Perhaps we were mistaken, it has been so long,
In the fierce purpose of these Dead Eye Dans?
Did they too wake at night, in a high fever,
And wonder when direction would be clear if ever?
– For the saint is the man most likely to do wrong.

In any case we later ones can only hope
For the positive landmark on the distant slope.
Moving through this dead world's Indian Nation
The heart must build its own direction –
Which only in the future has a permanent shape.

✦ SUCH SIMPLE LOVE

All night long I hear the sleepers toss
Between the darkened window and the wall.
The madman's whimper and the lover's voice,
The worker's whisper and the sick child's call –
Knowing them all

I'd walk a mile, maybe, hearing some cat
Crying its guts out, to throttle it by hand,
Such simple love I had. I wished I might –
Or God might – answer each call in person and
Each poor demand.

Well, I'd have been better off sleeping myself.
These fancies had some sentimental charm,
But love without direction is a cheap blanket
And even if it did no one any harm,
No one is warm.

✦ NOCTURNE MILITAIRE

Miami Beach: wartime

Imagine or remember how the road at last led us
Over bridges like prepositions, linking a drawl of islands.
The coast curved away like a question mark, listening slyly
And shyly whispered the insomniac Atlantic.
But we were uncertain of both question and answer,
Stiff and confused and bemused in expendable khaki,
Seeing with innocent eyes, the walls gleaming,
And the alabaster city of a rich man's dream.

Borne by the offshore wind, an exciting rumor,
The legend of tropic islands, caresses the coast like hysteria,
Bringing a sound like bells rung under sea;
And brings the infected banker and others whose tenure
Is equally uncertain, equally certain: the simple
And perfect faces of women – like the moon
Whose radiance is disturbing and quite as impersonal:
Not to be warmed by and never ample.

They linger awhile in the dazzling sepulchral city,
Delicately exploring their romantic diseases,
The gangster, the capitalist and their protegés
With all their doomed retainers:
                    not worth your hate or pity
Now that they have to learn a new language –
And they despise the idiom like an upper class foreigner:
The verb *to die* baffles them. We cannot mourn,
But their doom gives stature at last, moon-dazzled,
                    silhouette on the flaming Atlantic.

Something is dying. But in the fierce sunlight,
On the swanky golf-course drill-field, something is being born
Whose features are anonymous as a child's drawing
Of the lonely guard whose cry brings down the enormous night.
For the sentry moonlight is only moonlight, not
Easy to shoot by. But our devouring symbols

(Though we walk through *their* dying city
         and *their* moonlight lave us like lovers)
Are the loin-sprung spotlight sun and the hangman sack-hooded
        blackout.

       *   *   *

Now in the east the dark, like many waters,
Moves, and uptown, in the high hotels, those few
Late guests move through their remembered places
But their steps are curiously uncertain, like a sick man's
        or a sleepwalker's.
Down the beach, in rooms designed for their masters,
The soldiers curse and sing in the early blackout.
Their voices nameless but full of fear or courage
Ring like calm bells through their terrible electric idyll.

They are the nameless poor who have been marching
Out of the dark, to that possible moment when history
Crosses the tracks of our time. They do not see it approaching,
But their faces are strange with a wild and unnoticed mystery.
And now at the Casino the dancing is nice and no one
Notices the hunchback weeping among the bankers,
Or sees, like the eye of an angel, offshore, the burning tanker,
As the night patrol of bombers climbs through the rain and is gone.

✦ EMBLEMS OF EXILE

The hunchback in the park with halo of pigeons
Expelled from towers by the bells of noon
Is hunting in the gospel of accident the sign
Of the time (foretold) when, king of this pageant,
All shall wear humps on their backs but none
Approach the elegance which fits his own.
Through the window of normality the eyes are bold
With the emblem of exile on his shoulder.

Or examine the beggar in the empty street
On whom the hysteria of midnight falls:
In the bible of remembrance he rings all bells
But the doors are boundaries of his exiled state.
A prince of loneliness and drunken brawls
He calls the hours of conscience. Morning fills
The street with supplicants and he receives
Their bribes for silence and for short reprieves.

All these are symbols of bereavement, Love:
The moon is naked as a shivering harp,
The crutch, though it put forth the green branch of hope,
The telephone, the letter – tokens of leave.
And if I assume the beggar's or the hunchback's shape
It is that I lack your grace which blessed my heart
Before the war, before the long exile
Which the beggarman mind accepts but cannot reconcile.

✦ A LETTER FOR MARIAN

I sit musing, ten minutes from the Jap,
Six hours by sun from where my heart is,
Forty-three years into the hangman's century,
Half of them signed with the difficult homage
Of personal existence.

My candle is burning at both ends and the middle,
And my halo is blazing, but I'm blind as a bat.
If fortune knocks twice, no one will answer.
Am going on instruments, my private weather
Socked in zero zero.

Sorely troubled by the need for identity
And its best expression, communication.
But the lights fail on the hills, the voice is lost in
The night of the army, or even in death, its
Big fog.

When the telephone rings there's a war on each end.
The message arrives, but there's no one to sign for it.
No one can translate the songs of the birds or
The words on the radio where the ignorant enemy
Is jamming all frequencies.

The need is definition of private boundaries:
This hill is my heart: and these worn mountains
What honor remains: this forest, what courage;
Bounded by love and by need, my frontiers
Extend to include you;

Or the need to say: this is the word and this
Its easiest meaning – for the brave words are all now
Devoured by the small souls from within:
Politicos offer the embroidered noose:
"See if this fits you."

Needed between all men and all peoples
For history to turn on the pimp and the slaver
The eyes of the poor and their terrible judgment.
Simple as the lover says "I am yours."
But not so easy.

◆ CELEBRATION FOR JUNE 24

For Marian

Before you, I was living on an island
And all around the seas of that lonely coast
Cast up their imitation jewels, cast
Their fables and enigmas, questioning, sly.
I never solved them, or ever even heard,
Being perfect in innocence: unconscious of self;
Such ignorance of history was all my wealth –
A geographer sleeping in the shadow of virgins.

But though my maps were made of private countries
I was a foreigner in all of them after you had come,
For when you spoke, it was with a human tongue
And never understood by my land-locked gentry.
Then did the sun shake down a million bells
And birds bloom on bough in wildest song!
Phlegmatic hills went shivering with flame;
The chestnut trees were manic at their deepest boles!

It is little strange that nature was riven in her frame
At this second creation, known to every lover –
How we are shaped and shape ourselves in the desires of the other
Within the tolerance of human change.
Out of the spring's innocence this revolution,
Created on a kiss, announced the second season,
The summer of private history, of growth, through whose sweet sessions
The trees lift toward the sun, each leaf a revelation.

Our bodies, coupled in the moonlight's album
Proclaimed our love against the outlaw times

Whose signature was written in the burning towns.
Your face against the night was my medallion.
Your coming forth aroused unlikely trumpets
In the once-tame heart. They heralded your worth
Who are my lodestar, my bright and ultimate North,
Marrying all points of my personal compass.

This is the love that now invents my fear
Which nuzzles me like a puppy each violent day.
It is poor comfort that the mind comes, saying:
What is one slim girl to the peoples' wars?
Still, my dice are loaded: having had such luck,
Having your love, my life would still be whole
Though I should die tomorrow. I have lived it all.
– And love is never love, that cannot give love up.

♦ ENCOUNTER

At two thousand feet the sea wrinkles like an old man's hand.
Closer, in a monotone of peristalsis,
Its fugue-like swells create and recreate
One image in an idiot concentration.

From horizon to horizon, this desert
With the eye athirst for something stable
When off to southeast-ward –
It was a plane all right, or had been,
A shipside fighter, her pontoons floated her.
Smashed like a match-case, no one could be sure
If it were ours or had been one of theirs.

That's all there was. A thousand miles anywhere
There was only the north ocean, the poleward pallor,
Like a desolation of spirit, lonelier than god.
What did it mean? They thought of night fleets
In the ghostly boreal dark or maybe
Toy cardboard silhouettes in the bleak limbo of noon:
The salvos wink in bloom at twenty miles,
The pause, the roar like a night freight
And the near misses building their faery forests.

Where were these giants? The sea offered
A single clue, a symbol; no explanation.
Northward the fog banks thickened and on all horizons
As if jealous of giving up secured positions
The night stirred angrily like an old suspicion.

✦ BLUES FOR WARREN

killed spring 1942, North Sea

1.

The beasts in the schoolroom, whose transparent faces
Revealed the gesture in the hands of history,
Made love to us across calendars where lately
They'd planted minefields around our childhood mysteries.
We fell from innocence into the trap of the State,
From Blind Man's Buff and legends, stepped into the war of the Thirties.
Moving among the murders to the sound of broken treaties –
Shame of our kid's inexperience was all we knew at the start.

Opening at opportunity's knock –
That was the banker for our mortgaged love
That was the priest for our money or our life:
All this to teach us that nervous knack
A bourgeois culture keeps in stock –
Honest living in a thieves' society.
But under the academic acanthus, among the books and dubiety,
We summoned the value of man, his loss and luck.
Now, after alarums and plots, the obscure future –
The time which is Now – places awards and banners,
Emblems across our past; the time-shortened figures
Are decorated with light which none can feel.
And now we must condemn all those whose handsome dishonest features
Flowered on the stalk of our youth; their rentier manners
Calling alike to ruin and forgiveness
Placing across our lives their iron seal.

2.

Spotlight on midnight Europe: the furred boreal gleams
Of names on fallen monuments. A shaft of stallion's shriek
Nailed in the naked sheen of indifferent weather,
A weather of starvation. And among the ruins and the broken columns,
The betrayals, incrustations, the harps of the nineteenth century,
And among the treachery and hideous moneys of the world,
The Judas flags, the parliaments of beasts,
Devils with Oxford diplomas and diplomats' visas

He moved to the accompaniment of dispossessed angels:
The Angel of Love who issued no marriage licenses
The Angel of Reason with the brutal face of a child
The Angel of Hope who carried a gun in his fist
The Angel of the Fifth Season with his red flag
The Angel of Your Death who looks like your friend or your lover.
A kid knee-deep in the rotting dreams of dead statesmen,
In the First Imperialist War, thinking of home.

Home then after food queues and the cries of the starving
Lost like birds in the lord's infinite heaven
(Where no sparrow falls, etc.). But he wrote it down in his book,
Framed to remember: who were the false magicians;
What children had starved; what workers been murdered.
But what can a boy know in our time? The hawk wheels
An eye in the casual blue; the fox waits in the forest —
What can he know but the lost cries of the victims?

Down then to the matchless cold Atlantic,
Its oiled incredible reciprocating motion,
And the white ship, passage of hope, shape of return and departure
Gathered him into its hold like the sea's maw.
And the night came in like the sea's paw, gathering
The light away, and the ship, and the ocean's plunging mustangs.
By gullcry, by wavecry the littoral, the statues, the statements
The tide of the darkness gathers, are gathered into his heart.

To a barbaric rhythm of lights the seafarer slowly
Tammuz . . . Adonis, going away in the dark
With a few ears of maize, a wreath of barley leaves,
A bouquet of terror from Europe's autumn garden.
Return in Spring, or on Spring-side of ocean, America,
With the ritual wheat, with a dictionary of hopes;
Tammuz . . . Adonis . . . Warren . . . comes up the lordly Hudson
Bringing the summer in to the music of dancing light.

But the summer was unemployed that year —
June and July; and a million happinesses of weather,
Inventing lovers, filling all straights and flushes,
Knocked at the hearts where no one was at home.

At noon the roads ran over the hills like rabbits;
At midnight the clock's tongue spat out the clanging hours:
They ran to the dark interior, the back bush-country;
They fell at the feet of statues like a flight of iron flowers.

Those summers he rode the freights between Boston and Frisco
With the cargoes of derelicts, garlands of misery,
The human surplus, the interest on dishonor,
And the raw recruits of a new century.
The Boss's machine gun split open the human midnight
And the darkness bled its bland alarms and hours
Calling always to resistance and decision
Falling across his brief unhoused years.

3.

The bells of darkness gather their iron garlands
In the stone jungles of the blacked-out cities:
Now, after the lockout in Frisco, after the strike in New Orleans,
After the Wobblies, after the Communist Party,
After the Dorniers and Junkers, after the bomb with his number,
After the North Sea had him, after the ship went under.

The child's picture looks for itself in the old man's features,
Eye looks for sight; hand for its family fingers.
Our loves are memorialized in casual gestures
And the lost letter cries in the trunk at what it remembers.
Our loss weeps for itself, but it weeps without tongue or eyes
And the heart in its dark cave mourns. There is nothing to give it ease.

For the sea bird is not alone on the moonless waters,
Nor the fox alone in the high hills of the desert
Nor is even the soldier alone on his lone night watches
Holding with terrible integrity to his blind hazard.
The foxes have holes: the birds of the air their nests,
                and we will sometime go home,
But O in the timeless night, in the dark nothing, Warren, you are alone.

4.

These envy the wild birds; these, the shy life of the mole –
The blind night fugue of flight or the mothering cave in the hill.

These dream the fast fadeout, blessed by distance:
They see space as saviour, negation of form and identity,
                    an underground existence.
For these ran away at childhood, seeking a stranger's country
But arrived as the masked Prince or the son of southern gentry.
These others whose progressive alienation,
                    centripetal and strict,
Divorces the world instead of themselves,
                    prefer the abstract
And feuding heresy. They turn from the world and find
Health in their high foreheads, or their indifference to hope,
                    but their fond
Elaborate and humdrum disguises can never bandage their wounds.

These escape from themselves in the world; these others
                    from the world in themselves,
But are haunted by a small disquieting awareness that nothing saves –
The explorer who escapes geography, the hophead
                    who shoots up the town,
The sage on his pillar, the professor in his tower
                    where his thoughts go round and round –
They are shadowed by a sinister familiar they remember but
                    cannot place,
He appears in their nightmares; if they think of his name
                    they are certain to fall from grace.
And between one pole and the other, as between desire and desire,
The Socially Necessary Man is hanging in chains of fire.
(His candle burns for the saviour whose birthday is drawing near.)

Oh, hell has many doorways, the key is under the mat,
And a light is burning darkly for the wandering boy tonight.
And you yearn like a tramp under the happy window
Wanting the warmth and the voices and shelter from the wild winter.
But the final achievement of each is his own damnation;
There is a family devil attendant on every private notion.
To the saint withdrawn in himself, the hero in his passage of exile,
Comes the questioner they fear to remember:
                    and the terrible judgments fall.
For turning and turning in their monstrous hells of negation
They escape the glory and guilt of human action.

They haply escape salvation, escape the Fall.
But you, Warren, in the general affirmative hell
(Which includes all others) escaped these common infections
Avoiding Pride's Scylla, Fear's Charybdis, Hope's defection,
Though fiends with Kiwanis masks howled from their parlor lair,
Or tried to hold your hands across a war,
And the professors in their towers let down their long dark hair.

You moved in the light of your five angels as when the mythical great
Jesus, his common worker's clothes embroidered all over with hot
Big eyes of the poor and insulted moved on earth; or as later
Lenin arose again in the Finland Station
Thrones, Powers, Dominions, Soviets, Unions and Risings
Attended his coming and between two hells in fiery
Chains the Man of the Third Millennium stirred in his hell –

But the Fifth angel blows
And a star falls in the burning sea . . .

5.
A star falls in the sea. Beyond the window
The clocks of a thousand cities record their minute advantages.
The dawn wind lifts and the lawns of the Fifth decade
Prepare for a congress of sunlight. The workers awake,
Groaning to a day of sweat and statistics.

The early flowers make a fool of our Progress. The clocks condemn it.
But the lockout imposed by Natural Grace admits no scabs,
No hiding place down here and no retreat
Beyond the fence of apes, to the animals' innocence.
And we have given hostages to the shadowing future
(You Warren, and my brother, and the comrades
          in a hundred countries –
In the casualty lists all names are manifestoes)
And burnt offerings to the shocking, sublime
Instinct of brotherhood, the human desire for perfection.

Accept then, brother, this heavy burden,
This crucifixion we put upon you: Man
Who was, in the university in the lost South,

And among the poor in the middle hell of Europe,
And among the strikers in the American Winter,
And among the fighters in this long war
Who was in our sin and death and at the hour of our birth
Was, is now and ever shall be
Scapegoat and Saviour.

Therefore I praise you as one of whom death was required,
Who descended into hell for our sakes; awakener
Of the hanging man, the Man of the Third Millennium.
Who chose the difficult damnation and lived on that narrow margin
While the cries went up from the poor and it snowed in the churches
And hysterical roses mourned from the bankers' lapels.

A star falls in the sea. The darkness takes it, takes you –
As the sea of the primitives gathered their flowers and Adonis,
Leaving the sea knell only, a submarine tolling of bells –
Takes you to transmutations in the wild interior uplands,
Down fathomless dreaming funnels of the tides,
To new planes of struggle, levels of organization,
And the nodal point of qualitative change:
Toward a richer fulfillment, to more definitive capes,
Clamoring loud where on tomorrow's littoral reaches
Are beached the spring-tide flowers of our hopes.

◆ ARS POETICA:
OR: WHO LIVES IN THE IVORY TOWER?

Perhaps you'd like a marching song for the embattled prolet-
Ariat, or a realistic novel, the hopeful poet
Said, or a slice of actual life with the hot red heart's blood running,
The simple tale of a working stiff, but better than Jack London?

Nobody wants your roundelay, nobody wants your sestina,
Said the housewife, we want Hedy Lamarr and Gable at the cinema,
Get out of my technicolor dream with your tragic view and your verses;
Down with iambic pentameter and hurray for Louella Parsons.

Of course you're free to write as you please, the liberal editor answered,
But take the red flags out of your poem – we mustn't offend the censor –
And change this stanza to mean the reverse, and you must tone down
            this passage;
Thank God for the freedom of the press and a poem with a message!

Life is lousy enough without you should put it into a sonnet,
Said the man in the street, so keep it out of the novel, the poem, the drama;
Give us a paean of murder and rape, or the lay of a willing maiden,
And to hell with the Bard of Avalon and to hell with Eliot Auden.

Recite the damn things all day long, get drunk on smoke come Sunday,
I respect your profession as much as my own, but it don't pay off when
            you're hungry;
You'll have to carry the banner instead – said the hobo in the jungle –
If you want to eat; and don't forget: it's my bridge you're sleeping under.

Oh it's down with art and down with life and give us another reefer –
They all said – give us a South Sea isle, where light my love lies dreaming;
And who is that poet come in off the streets with a look unleal and lour?
Your feet are muddy, you son-of-a-bitch, get out of our ivory tower.

✦ A LITTLE SONG ABOUT CHARITY

(Tune of Matty Grove)

The boss came around at Christmas –
Oh smiling like a lamb –
He made me a present of a pair of gloves
And then cut off my hands –
Oh and then cut off my hands.

The boss came around on my birthday
With some shoes of a rich man's brand.
He smiled like a priest and he cut off my feet
Then he said: "Go out and dance" –
Oh he said: "Go out and dance."

The boss came around on May Day.
He said: "You may parade."
Then his cops shot us down in the open street
And they clubbed us into jail –
Oh they clubbed us into jail.

The preacher says on Sunday:
"Turn ye the other cheek."
Don't turn it to the boss on Monday morn:
He may knock out all your teeth –
Oh he may knock out your teeth.

So listen to me workers:
When the boss seems kind and good
Remember that the stain on the cutting tool
Is nothing but your blood –
Oh it's nothing but your blood.

If you love your wife and daughters,
And if you love your sons,
And if you love the working class
Then keep your love at home.
Don't waste it on the cockroach boss
But keep your love at home.

✦ A WARRANT FOR PABLO NERUDA

With the fury of cinders, with the despair of dusty
Great meat-eating birds stuffed under glass, with
The public stealth of rust on wedding rings,
The shriveled bureaucrats with flag-false eyes –
Smug as one-legged guides of the blind

Or politicians impersonating men –
Water their withered bible, loosen the night's black
Knife and now on the polo fields of the rich
Exercise the clanking hounds of illusion
And oil up a warrant for the twentieth century.

They are hunting for you, Neruda. And who now
Will stop them from stuffing the wild birds of the forest
With the blue fission of national neuroses? Who
Will found the myth of Copper? Who at Magellan's
Delta remember the ritual of forgiveness?

No one but you. No one but you. It is just.
They must hunt you, because of what they have forgotten:
The name of the buried miner. (The bronze face of wheat,
The river of indulgence that flowed from O'Higgins' side,
Dries in their heads like moss in a filing cabinet.)

And what of Bolivar's tears, curling like purple chips
From the lathes of usury? They go with you to the high
Andes where police cannot marshal a true man to hunt you –
No, though the Supreme Court, unhappily sane
And naked, run through the downtown streets, shouting

That laws have become just, black white, odd even –
No. The Conspiracy of October Lilacs is against them;
The Fronde of Innocence cocks a summer rifle;
The Union of Barley is on strike, and everywhere
An alchemy of resistance transmutes your flowering name.

◆ VISION OF THREE ANGELS
VIEWING THE PROGRESS OF SOCIALISM

And the first with his hands folded and a money belt for a truss
Said looking into the Commune: Well I will be damned and buggered,
Having been a banker in real life, to see how those burrowing beggars
Live without mortgages or rents and with no help from us.

And the second who had been a soldier in civilian life said: Jesus
Christ they'll never believe me when I tell the boys in the squad-room
That no one down there says sir, and they won't believe what's harder,
That even bughouse nuts don't want to be Julius Caesar.

And the third with the teamster's cap and callouses on his wing
Said I fell away from the flesh and into the hands of heaven
But the working stiffs down there are finally getting even
So I'll stick around until Judgment. Heaven is a sometime thing.

◆ BLUES FOR JIMMY

For Jimmy McGrath
Killed June 1945

1.

(If it were evening on a dead man's watch,
Flowerfall, sundown, the light furled on the pane;
And the shutters going up on the windows of the twentieth century,
6 Post Mortem in the world of the dead –)

    The train was late. We waited among the others,
    All of us waiting for friends on the late train.
    Meanwhile the usual darkness, the usual stars,
    Allies of the light trust and homeless lovers.
    And then the train with its clanking mechanical fury.
    "Our will could neither turn it around nor stop it."
    Abrupt as history it violates the station –
    The knife, the dream, the contemporary terror.

(Midnight awakens on a dead man's watch:
The two exact figures in the million beds
Embrace like skeletons chained in other dreams,
In the world of the dead where love has no dominion.)

    "And then we took him to the funeral parlor,
    Half-way house, after the train came in."
    We found he had put on another face,
    The indifferent face of death, its brutality and pallor.
    "And now at last, everyone is home?"
    All but you, brother. We left you there alone.

(The dead man's watch unlocks the naked morning,
And the day, already bandaging victories and wounds,
Assumes like Time the absolute stance of indifference,
On yesterday's sorrow setting its actual seal.)

    Among the absorbing tenants of god's half-acre
    We gave you back into the mundane chemistry.
    The banker dug the grave, but the grave and gentle
    Were part of the common plot. The priestly succor,

Scattering platitudes like wreaths of wilted flowers,
Drove in the coffin nails with god's own little hammer –
You are stapled still; and we are freed of onus.
Brother, te laudamus, hallowed be our shame.

(The shadow of noon – upon a dead man's watch –
Falls on the hours and mysteries; April, October
Darkening, and the forward and following centuries. The blind flyer
Locates himself on the map by that cone of silence.)

2.

Locates himself by that cone of silence,
But does not establish his private valence:
When the long grey hearse goes down the street
The driver is masked and his eyes are shut –
While confessing the dead man is his brother,
Only in dreams will admit the murder,
Accepting then what is always felt:
The massive implacable personal guilt.

Who refuses to be his brother's keeper
Must carry a knife and never sleep,
Defending himself at whatever cost
Against that blind importunate ghost.
Priest, banker, teacher or publican,
The mask of the irresponsible man
May hide from the masker his crimes of passion
But not the sin of his class position.

And what of the simple sensual man
Who only wants to be let alone,
With his horse and his hound and his house so fine,
A car and a girl and a voting machine?
Innocent Mr. and Mrs. Onan
Are dead before they have time to lie down.
The doorbell rings but they are away.
It is better to murder than deny.

The desperate laws of human motion
Deny innocence but permit salvation;

If we accept sentence before we are tried
We discover the crime our guilt had hid.
But the bourgeois, the saint, the two-gun man,
Who close the gates upon their dream,
Refuse to discover that of salvation
There is no private accumulation.

3.
The wind dies in the evening. Dust in the chill air
Settles in thin strata, taking the light with it,
Dusk before dusk in the river hollows.
And westward light glamors the wide Missouri,
The foothills, the Rockies, the arc of the harping coast.
And then the brooding continental night.

When I was a child the long evenings of midsummer
Died slow and splendid on my bedroom windowpane,
And I went into sleep's magnetic landscape
With no fear of awakening in a country of nightmares.

It was easy then. You could let the light go —
Tomorrow was another day and days were all the same:
Pictures in a book you'd read, segments of sealed and certain time:
Easy to go back to the day before yesterday, the year before last.

But now it is impossible. The leaf is there, and the light,
Fixed in the photograph, but the happiness is lost in the album,
And your words are lost in the mind, and your voice in the years,
And your letters' improbable tongues trouble the attic darkness.

And this is the true nature of grief and the human condition:
That you are nowhere; that you are nowhere, nowhere,
Nowhere on the round earth, and nowhere in time,
And the days like doors close between us, lock us forever apart.

4.
Not where spring with its discontinued annuities
Fills birds' nests with watches, dyes the winds yellow,
Scatters on the night its little flowers of disenchantment
And a drunken alphabet like the memory of clocks.

Not where summer, at the mercury's Feast of Ascension,
Deploys in fields the scarecrows of remembrance;
Summer with the wheat, oil, bread, birth, honey and barley,
And a hypnotised regiment of weeping butterflies.

Not when fall reopens private wounds
To stain the leaves and split the stones in walls;
Opening the doors on the furniture of false enigmas
And a mechanical patter of crazy magicians.

Not when winter on the buried leaf
Erects its barricades of coal stoves and forgetfulness;
With the warmth indoors, talk, love, camaraderie,
And outside a blizzard of years and corpses.

The calendar dies upon a dead man's watch. He is nowhere,
Nowhere in time. And yet must be in Time.
And when the Fifth Season with its mass and personal ascensions –
Fire-birds rising from the burning towns of Negation
Orbit toward freedom –
Until then, brother, I will keep your watch.

5.
I will not deny you through grief,
Nor in the masks and horrors of the voodoo man
Nor sell you in a mass for the dead
Nor seven out and forget you
Nor evict your spirit with a charming rune.
Nor wear my guilt for a badge like a saint or a bourgeois poet.

I forgive myself of your death: Blind shadow of my necessity –
Per mea culpa – cast by a son of freedom
I climb the hill of your absolute rebellion.
I do not exorcise you: you walk through the dark wood before me.

Though I give your loves to the hours,
Your bones to the first four seasons
Your hope to the ironies

Your eyes to the hawks of heaven
Your blood is made part of the general-strike fund
Your courage is coined into the Revolution
Your spirit informs the winds of the Fifth Season.

Only the tick of a watch divides us.
The crime is to deny the union of opposites.
I make your death my watch, a coin of love and anger,
With your death on one side and mine on the other.
Locked on my wrist to remember us by.

♦ TOURISTS AT ENSENADA

The sunlight, like Rouault, draws a line
At everything, but shadow seems as real
As its object – stricter, even, to its form
Than the wasted color of the worn stone.

The sea fringes a desert. Travellers come
Where the wave repeats itself in endless promise.
On the uplands are the shabby goats, lean pigs,
And the poor in their doorways, watching the roads

Where the tourists flash past. The peasant is eclipsed
By the solar procession of the rich and bored
Who find the poor fearsome, but the blackening jail
And American motels enclosed in white walls

Romantic. Disturbing, though, that black-and-white
Life. The cripple who rasps along the street
Like nails on a slate lines all the tourist ear
With cries as real and shadowy as foreign fear.

And a voice like a voice in dreams cried out in the stone wilderness,
Calling out of the whirlwind, sounding its gongs and thunders,
Saying: death to the four kings of indifference!
To all despoilers of sweat and virtue and
Death to the defamers of the sacrament of wheat!
Destroy the temples of these pious sinners!

> And the liberals said: Hush, mate, we know it is hard,
> And naturally we will help you, but you must be conscious
> Of the danger of letting the people know they've been had.
> For Christ's sake don't wake up that sleeping monster.

And the voice as a burning dove flew out of a blue Monday
With an iron curse in its throat like the spike of the morning whistle,
Saying: death to the three whores of history,
Church, state, and property, and those privileged coiners
Of the counterfeit currency of life! Level
The stations of compulsion, Time's stony circuits!

> And the hirelings said: Now shut your trap, Jack,
> You're beginning to sound like a man with his head under water.
> Lie back and relax and everything will be jake
> Or there'll be hell before breakfast and no snow all winter.

And the voice cried down like a bell from the ruined tower of conscience,
Shaking the chromium flowers in the garden of moral decrees,
Saying: death to the two nuns of coercion
Who steal the candy of childhood! Woe
To that subtle thief of youth, the nine-armed god
Of usury whose hands are in everyone's pockets!

And the doctor said with a slick shine in his eyes
And a skinful of junk: Lie down and count to twenty.
And he turned to the banker and said: Knife and forceps, please.
And they broke into the body without warrant of entry.

But the voice cried like a trumpet from the nave of the slashed throat;
The heart leaped out of the broken trench of his breast and shouted!
Out of the ports of his eyes flew the hawks of the first four seasons:
Born from his dreaming blood was the red flag of the fifth.

✦ THE LITTLE ODYSSEY OF JASON QUINT, OF SCIENCE, DOCTOR

1.

Betrayed by his five mechanic agents, falling
Captive to consciousness, he summons light
To all its duties, and assumes the world
Like a common penance. Rust on the green tongue burns
Like history's corrosive on his living tree.
But all the monsters of his sleep's dark sea
Are tame familiars in the morning sun.

2.

He sees the nation browse across burnt miles
Of toast, toward the time-clock. Deafened, hears
A Gettysburg of breakfast food explode
Against the surd tympanum of the air.
The roads outside to No-and-Any Where
Trigger all space-time to a zero Now.
The punctual goddess blossoms on his brow –
Pragmatic emblem of the daylit need.

3.

Now with his thought the rank and maundy world
(That lost between quanta and mechanic wave
All pulp and passion sprawls around the globe)
He stiffens, as a hand informs a glove,
And drags each lank potential into form.
Thus the hieratic arrow of his glance
Creates St. Sebastian Avenue Street Place –
All of sublunary circumstance
Crowds on the casual platform of his gaze.

4.

Like money sealed in a pneumatic tube
He whirls beneath the city's stony floor
To where the cold coordinates of work
Advance their cross-hairs on the target hour.
There surplus value's mathematic flower

(All X squared Y squared like a tesseract
Or ghostly dirigible) grows unseen
Across the lean dimension of in fact.

5.

Grows all unseen as Jason Quint pursues
The windy hazard of the Absolute
Through icy tundras, farther than the Horn,
Vaster than Asia in their wuthering snows.
The sweat of progress and humanity
Colors no litmus in those latitudes;
In a rustle of banknotes and casualty lists
The Bomb is shaken from the wrath-bearing tree.

6.

The quitting whistle lofts a flag of truce,
And all hope's flutes and harpsichords compound
The lonely leisure. The Great Nocturnal Drift
Sets to its Deep. He walks the park. Profound
Unease returns to Quint. The sleepy lathes
Of hummingbirds machine the emerald
Of garden silence which his feet confuse.
The statues hoist, on labyrinthine paths,
The mineral grandeur of a public smile.

7.

And the world goes blank, and heavy as a stone
Rolls into night. It is the human hour.
Imperfect. Lovers, food and politics
Command the air, and Jason Quint alone,
Clothed in abstraction, like a bush that burns
In the blind frequencies where none may pass,
Stalks through that only country of the poor –
The lamplit hour the quitting whistle mourns.

8.

Imperfect. The stability of dextrous stars
Offers him comfort, but their light is cold.
A storm of sentiment, sudden as a cloud
Of migrant birds, sings in his head. Now stirs
The terrible friend, companion of his dreams,
With his emotional algebra of need and loss –
The hateful witness to his mortal part
And confirmation of his loneliness.

✦ MEMORIAL

for Jimmy McGrath

Nothing prolongs. Neither the bronze plaque
Of graveyard splendor, nor public memorial. Even
The watery eye of memory, weeping its darlings back
Fails them. Flung like leaves on the cold heaven
In Time's own season, that Always when totals are taken,
        And the mortal tree is shaken,
            So, from its riven,
        Blood-branched and bony haven,
The soul is blown toward that South where only the dead awaken.

Nothing arouses. Shrouded in marble snow
He enters the house of his fatal opposite, under
His careless star, and the statues. The bedded seeds outgrow
Their sleepy winter, but now there is no Spring thunder
Can shock him awake, who, lying companioned and lonely
        In his small house, can only –
            Against Time's yonder –
        Live nigh as a bloodless wonder
In the chinese box of the mind, a mummied guest in
                that haunted and homely

Dark where nothing endures. Though the heart entomb
And hold that weakling ghost for a season, the altering
Cold years like snow blindfold our love, as time
Darks a stone angel. So does memory, faltering,
Kill you again – your stillness is whirled and hurried
        To nature's wilder order.
            It is the faulting
        Heart in that bloody welter
Fails you and fails. Forgive this second murder.

◆ ODE FOR THE AMERICAN DEAD IN ASIA

1.

God love you now, if no one else will ever,
Corpse in the paddy, or dead on a high hill
In the fine and ruinous summer of a war
You never wanted. All your false flags were
Of bravery and ignorance, like grade school maps:
Colors of countries you would never see –
Until that weekend in eternity
When, laughing, well armed, perfectly ready to kill
The world and your brother, the safe commanders sent
You into your future. Oh, dead on a hill,
Dead in a paddy, leeched and tumbled to
A tomb of footnotes. We mourn a changeling: you:
Handselled to poverty and drummed to war
By distinguished masters whom you never knew.

2.

The bee that spins his metal from the sun,
The shy mole drifting like a miner ghost
Through midnight earth – all happy creatures run
As strict as trains on rails the circuits of
Blind instinct. Happy in your summer follies,
You mined a culture that was mined for war:
The state to mold you, church to bless, and always
The elders to confirm you in your ignorance.
No scholar put your thinking cap on nor
Warned that in dead seas fishes died in schools
Before inventing legs to walk the land.
The rulers stuck a tennis racket in your hand,
An Ark against the flood. In time of change
Courage is not enough: the blind mole dies,
And you on your hill, who did not know the rules.

3.

Wet in the windy counties of the dawn
The lone crow skirls his draggled passage home:
And God (whose sparrows fall aslant his gaze,
Like grace or confetti) blinks and he is gone,
And you are gone. Your scarecrow valor grows
And rusts like early lilac while the rose
Blooms in Dakota and the stock exchange
Flowers. Roses, rents, all things conspire
To crown your death with wreaths of living fire.
And the public mourners come: the politic tear
Is cast in the Forum. But, in another year,
We will mourn you, whose fossil courage fills
The limestone histories: brave: ignorant: amazed:
Dead in the rice paddies, dead on the nameless hills.

✦ THE REPEATED JOURNEY

for Marian

Again and again I make the intolerable journey:
First three days in the locked train, passing my home
On the stormy midnight when no light burns and all the houses
Are shut: then pinesmell, rain, confusion, a cold camp;
Again and again

I make the winter voyage: first the narrow
Sea-passage between the mountains where like frozen
Smoke the waterfalls hang and the scenery becomes portentous,
Dream-like and sullen, charged with a higher reality
Than our own; then, shadowy

As clouds in the roaring night-black ocean, islands
Plunge, fog-bound, nameless; finally, driving
Seaward, the headlands, and the crooked harbor: wreckage,
Spume like spiders crawling, gun-metal water;
Again and again

I climb the hill: past the cemetery, the dead
Fighter aircraft, past the shops where the great
Machines rust in their beds and know it is
Useless, useless, the night-journey inbound and cannot,
Can not turn back –

What am I hunting? I cannot remember. Rain
Slats like shot on the empty tents. The flaps
Are all closed tight on nothing. On ghosts. The night
Comes screaming down on the wind. Boredom. Loneliness.
Again and again

I return to the hunt for something long buried
In Time, like the dead in the cliff-face cemetery.
Loneliness, terror of death, splendor of living –
I rescued these wounded: but cannot reclaim my youth
Nor those lost violent years whose casual ignorant lovers
We were for a season.

◆ THE WORLD OF THE PERFECT TEAR

for Jimmy McGrath, killed 1945

Fire from a fixèd star
Locates no place you are.
No warmth left in the air
Reminds that you were there.
Everything you were
Is canceled in the earth
And memory's single tear
Drowns all your footprints here.

Yet in that crystal sphere
All is reflected clear –
Though no one can stand tall
Where earth itself is small
And fire is cool and air
Thinner than breath. Still, there,
The elements prevail
Reduced in memory's scale.

Sad joke: to entomb you here
In the damp world of a tear –
Though we navigate that globe
With a Magellan love.
Still, more like the Flood, this drop –
Or dead man's Ark! – will whirl
And whelm the dying world:
To raise the living up.

✦ THE TROUBLE WITH THE TIMES

for Naomi Replansky

In this town the shops are all the same:
Bread, bullets, the usual flowers
Are sold but no one – no one, no one
Has a shop for angels,
No one sells orchid bread, no one
A silver bullet to kill a king.

No one in this town has heard
Of fox-fire rosaries – instead
They have catechisms of filthy shirts,
And their god goes by on crutches
In the stench of exhaust fumes and dirty stories.

No one is opening – even on credit –
A shop for the replacement of lost years.
No one sells treasure maps. No one
Retails a poem at so much per love.

No. It is necessary
To go down to the river where the bums at evening
Assemble their histories like cancelled stamps.
There you may find, perhaps, the purple
Weather, for nothing; the blue
Apples, free; the reddest
Antelope, coming down to drink at the river,
Given away.

◆ THE PROGRESS OF THE SOUL

Where once I loved my flesh,
That social fellow,
Now I want security of bone
And cherish the silence of my skeleton.

Where once I walked the world
Hunting the devil,
Now I find the darkness and the void
Within my side.

First to be good, then to be happy I
Worked and prayed.
Before the midnight, like the foul fiend,
I killed my dear friend.

Hope unto hope, dream beyond monstrous dream
I sought the world.
Now, at the black pitch and midnight of despair,
I find it was always here.

◆ PERPETUAL MOTION

One, one
Lives all alone,
Shape of the body's
Tree of bone.

Two, two
Can make the world do;
In youth, in youth,
But not in truth.

Three, three
And the body tree
Fades in the forest
Of company.

Three, three
Society,
Will do, will do,
But not for two

Since two, two
In love, withdraw;
Wish to be one,
To live alone,

But all must come
To the skeleton,
And one and one
Live all alone.

✦ LEGENDARY PROGRESS

When, in the darkness of his dream,
He felt the beast scream in his side
Shuddering to be born again
He crouched in the haunted, shadowy cave.

When twin colossi gripped the East
And rived the mystical world apart,
The rage and fire of a cold star
Kindled the darkness at his heart.

When darkness settled on the West
He heard the beast laugh in his home.
The flesh sickened on the bone.
He sought the cold, monastic heaven.

When the beast was partly freed
Hunger of voyage shook the world.
Toward Magellanic darkness driven
He gyved the mystical world in one.

When to perfection of the One
He drove his cold and careless thought
The beast screamed in his terror of
The frozen heaven of the absolute.

When Progress in its cold machine
Drove all the terror from the wood
The fury chained in the drowsy blood
Convulsed at the metal smell of sin.

When in terror of the beast
He prayed protection for his dream.
A cold chaotic darkness came;
He crouched in the shadowy haunted cave.

Now twin colossi rive the world
The starship drops its furious rime.
The terror out of the darkness comes.
The beast is raging in its time.

◆ IN PRAISE OF NECESSITY

Nostalgia of old men,
That spends itself in the sun
Hunting the vanished Sioux
Or shooting the buffalo down,
Is ground-rent to the Past,
Shafts of whose vanquished years
Pierce all decadent men
To envenom new-born desires.
Thus the blind demands of the heart
Are thwarted by out-lived lives –
The Wise Man's experience is
The wisdom of killing the tribes.

How could it be otherwise?
All that's alive in the Past
Fastens itself on death,
Since to live is to change. Turned ghost
It is clothed in the future and us –
Not bound, traditional men
Remembering ritual words
Learned when their meaning was gone.
Shamans around a fire
Where tired Ghost Dancers sway
Pray back the lost buffalo herds –
Words for a vanished age.

Then praise the hunters, who
Through yesterday's cold camps
(Where banked-up spirit-fires,
Ice-flamed, will warm no hand)
Advance to break new trail
Impatient of the mean-
ingless dreams of legend herds,
Words of the old men;
And praise necessity
That frees the past of its snares,
Praising the killer heart
That makes dead meat of the years.

◆ AGAINST THE FALSE MAGICIANS

for Don Gordon

The poem must not charm us like a film:
See, in the war-torn city, that reckless, gallant
Handsome lieutenant turn to the wet-lipped blonde
(Our childhood fixation) for one sweet desperate kiss
In the broken room, in blue cinematic moonlight –
Bombers across that moon, and the bombs falling,
The last train leaving, the regiment departing –
And their lips lock, saluting themselves and death:
And then the screen goes dead and all go home . . .
Ritual of the false imagination.

The poem must not charm us like the fact:
A warship can sink a circus at forty miles,
And art, love's lonely counterfeit, has small dominion
Over those nightmares that move in the actual sunlight.
The blonde will not be faithful, nor her lover ever return
Nor the note be found in the hollow tree of childhood –
This dazzle of the facts would have us weeping
The orphaned fantasies of easier days.

It is the charm which the potential has
That is the proper aura for the poem.
Though ceremony fail, though each of your grey hairs
Help string a harp in the landlord's heaven,
And every battle, every augury,
Argue defeat, and if defeat itself
Bring all the darkness level with our eyes –
It is the poem provides the proper charm,
Spelling resistance and the living will,
To bring to dance a stony field of fact
And set against terror exile or despair
The rituals of our humanity.

✦ YOU CAN START THE POETRY NOW,
OR: NEWS FROM CRAZY HORSE

*– I guess all I'm trying to say is I saw Crazy Horse die for
        a split level swimming pool in a tree-house owned by
                a Pawnee-Warner Brothers psychiatrist about three
                        hundred feet above –*

You can start the poetry now.

*– above City Hall kind of sacred ground where they shot the Great
        Buddha wild drags in the atomic parking lot but no good
                gas seems I remember –*

You can Start the Poetry now.

*– remember John Grass, University of North Dakota '69, did not
        complete his thesis sort of half-classed Indian was too busy
                fighting Custer to write he wrote last of the ten
                        million Mohicanos when the physicists began changing red-
                                skins to greenbacks it wasn't*

YOU can Start the Poetry NOW!

*– wasn't Gall who built all those slaveways after lifting the weight
        of the guilt hair Custer's wasn't it Gall or Crazy
                Horse Sitting Bull or Rain-In-The-Face wigged him it was
                        later they died on the tailfins it makes you want to shoot horse-
                                power capitalists who done it –*

YOU CAN START the POETRY now ! !

*– who done it it's between the gilt heir and the surplus value
        grand cost of counting coup in the swimming pools stolen from
                the Teton Sioux first ones I ever saw with built-in jails it's
                        capitalism unlimited the american Platonic year what I
                                can't get straight is the white antelope they're using for
                                        money it's the –*

START THE POETRY! START THE POETRY NOW ! !

— it's the quarters and halves or maybe the whole antelope Buck that
gets me it's the cutting up of the Buffalo Bread it's all them
goddam swimming pools full of shot horses it's Christ Indians
and revolutionaries charging full-tilt at the psychiatrists'
couches and being blasted with the murderous electrical hot
missionary money of hell-by-installments it's all of us pining
and starving surrounded by the absolute heavenly pemmican-
charisma that Geronimo invented it's the —
START THE POETRY ! ! GODDAMN IT ! !
START THE POETRY ! ! START THE POETRY NOW ! !

✦ THE BUFFALO COAT

I see him moving, in his legendary fleece,
Between the superhighway and an Algonquin stone axe;
Between the wild tribes, in their lost heat,
And the dark blizzard of my Grandfather's coat;
Cold with the outdoor cold caught in the curls,
Smelling of the world before the poll tax.

And between the new macadam and the Scalp Act
They got him by the short hair; had him clipped
Who once was wild – and all five senses wild –
Printing the wild with his hoof's inflated script
Before the times was money in the bank,
Before it was a crime to be so mild.

But history is a fact, and moves on feet
Sharper than his, toward wallows deeper than.
And the myth that covered all his moving parts,
Grandfather's time had turned into a coat;
And what kept warm then, in the true world's cold
Is old and cold in a world his death began.

◆ RETURN TO MARSH STREET

Easter, 1959

1.

Twice, now, I've gone back there, like a part-time ghost
To the wrecked houses and the blasted courts of the dream
Where the freeway is pushing through.

        Snake country now.

         Rats-run –

Bearable, bearable –
Winos' retreat and the midnight newfound lands –
Bearable, perfectly bearable –
Of hungering rich lovers under the troubling moon
Their condominium;

      bowery close; momentary

           kingdom come –

Wild country of love that exists before the concrete
Is poured.

    Squatters there.

       That's all

O.K. with me.

2.

First time I went there – about a year ago come Monday –
I went hunting flowers: flowering bushes, flowering shrubs, flowering
Years-grown-over gardens: what was transportable.
What was transportable had been taken long away.
Among the detritus, rock-slides, confessions, emotional moraines –
Along the dream plazas and the alleys of the gone moon –
Some stragglers and wildlings: poppy, sorrel, nightblooming
Nothing.

    And found finally my own garden – where it had been –
A pissed-upon landscape now, full of joy-riding
Beer cans and condoms all love's used up these days
Empty wine bottles wrappers for synthetic bread

      . . . . . .

Larkspur, lupin, lavender, lantana, linaria, lovage.
And the foxglove's furry thimble and the tiny chime of fuchsia

All gone.
          The children's rooms have a roof of Nothing
And walls of the four wild winds.
                 And, in the rooms of the night,
The true foundation and threshing floor of love,
Are the scars of the rocking bed, and, on certain nights, the moon.
Unending landscape . . .
            dry . . .
                blind robins . . .*

3.

Blind Robins, Blind Robins – Fisherman, do you take Blind Robins
In the stony trough of the dry Los Angeles river?
No charmed run of alewives or swarming of holy mackerel
From the pentecostal cloud chambers of the sex-charged sea, no
Leaping salmon on the light-embroidered ladders of eternal redemption?
Damnation of blind robins . . .
              bacalao . . .
                 dried cod, is that
Is that all you take on your dead-rod green-fishing Jonah,
Poor boy, mad clean crazy lad I pulled once from this river in
                   spate it is not
Bearable.

4.

Well, wait, then.
          Observe.
               Sky-writing pigeons, their . . .
Blue unanswerable documents of flight, their . . .
Unearthly attachments.
          Observe:
             these last poor flowers,
               their light-shot promises,
That immortality, green signature of their blood . . .
          . . . . . .

* *Blind Robins are a smoked salt fish.*

Now, instantly, the concrete comes: the freeway leaps over the dead
River and this once now twice-green moment into the astonished
Suburbs of the imaginary city petrified
Megalopolitan grief homesteads of lost angels anguish . . .

On this day nothing rises from the dead, the river
Dying, the dry flowers going under the mechanic stone . . .
                                                        Sirs!
Archaeologists! what will you find at that level of ancient light?
Poverty destroyed sweet hearts and houses once before Progress
                                                        His Engines
Put down a final roof on the wild kitchens of that older
Order.
        These lovers long are fled into the storm.
        The river is dry.
                    It is finally.
                                completely.

Bearable

✦ PROVERBS OF THE MIDDLE WORLD

The perfect swan upon the perfect lake
Doubles its heaven in a single look.

* * *

No wise man can distinguish whore from prude
When they're wrapped in the common colors of their pride.

* * *

Some mask with courage, some with fear;
The rich wear power as a beast its fur.

* * *

The man of conscience or the man of sin —
All shadows take their color from the sun.

* * *

Who builds his freedom on another's life
Must start and tremble when his subjects laugh.

* * *

When queens of love proclaim their discontent,
The courts of lust shall judge the innocent.

✦ AH . . . TO THE VILLAGES!

Leaving the splendid plaza and the esplanade –
The majestic façades of metropolitan unease –
Let us to the vast savannahs of despair
Repair; and let us seek
The panoramas of malaise, the continental anguish,
The hysteria and the nausea of the villages.

      Somewhere – perhaps where Omaha, like a disease,
      And the magnificent, brumal names of Fargo, of Kalamazoo,
      Infect the spirit with magnificent ennui –
      A baroque splendor attends our small distress:
      We dress in the grand extravaganza of cafard.

      Still, there will come evenings without true discontent –
      The sparrows loud in the dust and the crows gone cawing home
      To the little wood; the lights ending at the prairie, and –
      As the divine and healing night comes down –
      The town reeling, unreasonably content.

In the one-horse town they have eaten the horse – allons!
But soft! Here are not only the megrims of small forms
And the subliminal melancholy of the central square.
Take care; for here you find
An intermontane anguish in the wind that sings you home:
Here is a false front distinguished as your own.

And contentment is momentary in the villages.

✦ A COAL FIRE IN WINTER

Something old and tyrannical burning there.
(Not like a wood fire which is only
The end of a summer, or a life)
But something of darkness: heat
From the time before there was fire.
And I have come here
To warm that blackness into forms of light,
To set free a captive prince
From the sunken kingdom of the father coal.

A warming company of the cold-blooded –
These carbon serpents of bituminous gardens,
These inflammable tunnels of dead song from the black pit,
This sparkling end of the great beasts, these blazing
Stone flowers diamond fire incandescent fruit.
And out of all that death, now,
At midnight, my love and I are riding
Down the old high roads of inexhaustible light.

✦ USED UP

1.

I remember the new-dropped colts in the time when I was a boy:
The steam of their bodies in the cold morning like a visible soul,
And the crimped hairy ring of warmed grass, first circle of sleep.
Spider-legged, later, they ate sugar from my shaken, scary hand.

2.

In a few more years they were broken: their necks were circled
With a farmer's need: with the dead leather legends and collars
                                        of their kin.
Gelded, the wild years cut out of them, harnessed to the world,
They walk the bright days' black furrows and gilded seasons of use.

3.

Now, dead; swung from the haymow track with block and tackle:
Gut-slit, blood in a tub for pigs, their skin dragged over
Their heads by a team of mules. Circlet of crows:
                        coyote song:
                                and bones
Rusting coulee moonlight: lush greenest spring grass where the body
Leaped.
            Three acts and death.
                        The horse
                                    rides
Into the earth.

◆ PRAISES

The vegetables please us with their modes and virtues.
                                        The demure heart
Of the lettuce inside its circular court, baroque ear
Of quiet under its rustling house of lace, pleases
Us.
        And the bold strength of the celery, its green Hispanic
¡Shout! its exclamatory confetti.
                                And the analogue that is Onion:
Ptolemaic astronomy and tearful allegory, the Platonic circles
Of His inexhaustible soul!
                                O and the straightforwardness
In the labyrinth of Cabbage, the infallible rectitude of Homegrown Mushroom
Under its cone of silence like a papal hat —
                                        All these
Please us.
            And the syllabus of the corn,
                                that wampum,
                                                its golden
Roads leading out of the wigwams of its silky and youthful smoke;
The nobility of the dill, cool in its silences and cathedrals;
Tomatoes five-alarm fires in their musky barrios, peas
Asleep in their cartridge clips,
                                beetsblood,
                                        colonies of the imperial
Cauliflower, and the buddha-like seeds of the pepper
Turning their prayerwheels in the green gloom of their caves.
All these we praise: they please us all ways: these smallest virtues.
All these earth-given:
                        and the heaven-hung fruit also . . .
                                                As instance
Banana which continually makes angelic ears out of sour
Purses, or the winy abacus of the holy grape on its cross
Of alcohol, or the peach with its fur like a young girl's —
All these we praise: the winter in the flesh of the apple, and the sun
Domesticated under the orange's rind.

                    We praise
By the skin of our teeth, Persimmon, and Pawpaw's constant
Affair with gravity, and the proletariat of the pomegranate
Inside its leathery city.
                    And let us praise all these
As they please us: skin, flesh, flower, and the flowering
Bones of their seeds: from which come orchards: bees: honey:
Flowers, love's language, love, heart's ease, poems, praise.

✦ DRIVING TOWARD BOSTON I RUN ACROSS ONE OF ROBERT BLY'S OLD POEMS

1.

Tonight we are driving past Lac Qui Parle toward Boston.
When I think of Boston ladies I am suddenly galvanic with joy!
I see them lying there, pale with Love . . . like flowers . . . like palimpsests!
On which we can still make out a few marginal words . . .
Wampum . . . rackrent . . . pui ine o dromos sto horyo, asshole!
Ah – the lemon ladies and the lime-green ladies of Boston!

2.

The parlors of those houses on the road to Boston are full of salt.
These ladies have taken the sea to bed just once too often . . .
And the men – ah, here the Cabots and the Lodges and Lowells are dozing
(Dreaming of rum and molasses, dreaming of Sacco and Vanzetti)
In an oily torpor, like the sleep of ancient Cadillacs . . .
Alas! John Adams: desuetude has entered the timing-chains of those
        enormous engines!

3.

Driving toward Boston we pass the Stuffed Ski Surf Shop –
And then the Stuffed Ski Surf Shop – again and again!
Perhaps we are not driving toward Boston after all . . .
Waltham flies by, full of mysterious time zones . . .
I know Boston is on the Post Road someplace in the nineteenth century.
The wind is whistling a snatch in the puritan winefield.
I speed forward, confident, thinking of the Boston ladies;
A little of last year's blue blood dreams and screams in the ditch.
Comforted, I press on – and on – perfectly happy.

4.

Whether or not we *are* heading toward Boston
(And even the question of whether I'm *perfectly* happy)
I leave to another time – a time full of lakes – and crickets!
Meanwhile I drive past Waltham again, gaining more time,
Somewhere on the road to or away from Boston . . .
Thinking of the Boston ladies I have a powerful erection!
High as the Dakota mountains! High as the great mountain near Fargo!

✦ TWO SONGS FROM
"THE HUNTED REVOLUTIONARIES"

for Henry Winston

1.

He imagines the great demons of
the four corners of his country

The violent darkness claims us all:
The indifferent demon of the North
Sends his abstract anguish forth,
Tall as you are and more tall.
The violent darkness claims us all.

Tall as you are and more tall,
The impotent demon of the South
Tears the tongue from the honest mouth.
The violent darkness claims us all,
Tall as you are and more tall.

The violent darkness claims us all:
The mechanical demon of the East —
The inflated demon of the West —
Tall as you are and more tall,
The violent darkness claims us all.

The violent darkness claims us all:
Now all your angels summon forth,
From East and West and South and North,
Tall as you are, and more tall.

2.

He calls upon the powers of earth

The dark is in love with forms of light.
Angel of conscience of the North,
Assure all mortals mortal worth!

Stars shine clearest in darkest night:
I summon the angel of the North.

Stars shine clearest in darkest night.
O randy angel of the South,
Be lust of joy in the fields of sloth!
An indifferent joy is man's secret fate:
I summon the angel of the South.

An indifferent joy is our secret fate.
Anarchic angel of the West,
In solidarity bind what's loosed!
All bitterness in time grows sweet:
I summon the angel of the West.

All bitterness in time grows sweet.
Shepherding angel of the East,
Organize concord in the breast!
The dark is in love with forms of light:
I summon the angel of the East.

The dark is in love with forms of light,
Tall as you are and more tall.
Though the violent darkness claim us all
An indifferent joy is our secret fate.
The stars shine clearest in darkest night.
All bitterness in time grows sweet.

✦ PROLETARIAN IN ABSTRACT LIGHT

Now on the great stage a silence falls.
In the long shudder toward collapse and birth,
There enters, singing, the muffled shape of a future.
He has no face; his hands are bloody;
He is for himself; he is not to please you.

> *You have stolen my labor*
> *You have stolen my name*
> *You have stolen my mystery*
> *You have stolen the moon*

The coldness of song goes on in his barbarous tongue.
The hours condense like snow. The marble weight
Of his dream, like a heavy cloud, leans on your glass houses.
Expropriated of time, he begins himself in *his* name;
He stamps his null on your day; the future collapses toward him:

> *I do not want your clocks*
> *I do not want your God*
> *I do not want your statues*
> *I do not want your love*

✦ READING THE NAMES OF
THE VIETNAM WAR DEAD

For a long day and a night we read the names:
Many thousand brothers fallen in the green and distant land . . .

Sun going south after the autumn equinox.
By night the vast moon: "Moon of the Falling Leaves";

Our voices hoarse in the cold of the first October rains.
And the long winds of the season to carry our words away.

The citizens go on about their business.
By night sleepers condense in the houses grown cloudy with dreams.
By day a few come to hear us and leave, shaking their heads
Or cursing. On Sunday the moral animal prays in his church.

It is Fall; but a host of dark birds flies toward the cold North.
Thousands of dense black stones fall forever through the
                darkness under the earth.

✦ SOMETHING IS DYING HERE

In a hundred places in North Dakota
Tame locomotives are sleeping
Inside the barricades of bourgeois flowers:
Zinnias, petunias, johnny-jump-ups –
Their once wild fur warming the public squares.

Something is dying here.
                     And perhaps I, too –
My brain already full of the cloudy lignite of eternity . . .

I invoke an image of my strength.
                            Nothing will come.
Oh – a homing lion perhaps
                       made entirely of tame bees;
Or the chalice of an old storage battery, loaded
With the rancid electricity of the nineteen thirties
Cloud harps iconographic blood
Rusting in the burnt church of my flesh . . .

But nothing goes forward:
The locomotive never strays out of the flower corral
The mustang is inventing barbwire the bulls
Have put rings in their noses . . .

The dead here
Will leave behind a ring of autobodies,
Weather-eaten bones of cars where the stand-off failed –

    Strangers: go tell among the Companions:
    These dead weren't put down by Cheyennes or Red Chinese:
    The poison of their own sweet country has brought them here.

✦ POLITICAL SONG FOR THE YEAR'S END

1.

The darkness of the year begins,
In which we hunt the summer kings.
(Who will kill Cock Robin when
His breast is cheery with his sin?)
And when, transfigured in the skies,
The starry, hunted hero dies,
The redemptive rain of his golden blood
Quickens the barley of the Good.
Sing to the moon, for every change must come.

2.

The democratic senator
's conjunctive to the warrior star,
And Market wavers into trine
As the geared heavens tick and shine.
The Worker snores; the Poet drowses
Through all his literary Houses;
The Goose hangs high, the Wife lays low,
And all the children are on Snow.
Sing to the moon, for every change is known.

3.

Each role must change. Each change must come.
Turning, we make the great Wheel turn
In a rage of impotence, forth and back
Through the stations of history's zodiac.
Caught in the trap of our daily bread,
A hopeful, stumbling multitude,
We surrender and struggle, save and slay,
Turning the Wheel in the ancient way.
Sing to the moon; for every change must pass.

4.

And now with an indifferent eye
We see our savior hunted by,
Into that furious dark of time
His only death may all redeem.
And when at last that time is grown
When all the great shall be cast down,
We rejoice to praise who now is slain —
For the darkness of the year is come.
Sing to the moon, for every change is known.

✦ GONE AWAY BLUES

Sirs, when you are in your last extremity,
When your admirals are drowning in the grass-green sea,
When your generals are preparing the total catastrophe –
I just want you to know how you can not count on me.

    I have ridden to hounds through my ancestral halls,
    I have picked the eternal crocus on the ultimate hill,
    I have fallen through the window of the highest room,
    But don't ask me to help you 'cause I never will.

Sirs, when you move that map-pin how many souls must dance?
I don't think all those soldiers have died by happenstance.
The inscrutable look on your scrutable face I can read at a glance –
And I'm cutting out of here at the first chance.

    I have been wounded climbing the second stair,
    I have crossed the ocean in the hull of a live wire,
    I have eaten the asphodel of the dark side of the moon,
    But you can call me all day and I just won't hear.

O patriotic mister with your big ear to the ground,
Sweet old curly scientist wiring the birds for sound,
O lady with the Steuben glass heart and your heels so rich and round –
I'll send you a picture postcard from somewhere I can't be found.

    I have discovered the grammar of the Public Good,
    I have invented a language that can be understood,
    I have found the map of where the body is hid,
    And I won't be caught dead in your neighborhood.

O hygienic inventor of the bomb that's so clean,
O lily white Senator from East Turnip Green,

O celestial mechanic of the money machine –
I'm going someplace where nobody *makes your scene.*

   Good-by, good-by, good-by,
   Adios, au 'voir, so long,
   Sayonara, dosvedanya, ciao,
   By-by, by-by, by-by.

✦ EPITAPH

Again, traveller, you have come a long way led by that star.
But the kingdom of the wish is at the other end of the night.
May you fare well, compañero; let us journey together joyfully,
Living on catastrophe, eating the pure light.

from

✦ PASSAGES TOWARD THE DARK ✦

✦ DAWN SONG

The city lifts toward heaven from the continent of sleep
This skin of bricks,
                            these wounds,
                                                    this soul of smoke and anguish,
These walls held up by hope and want, these right angles
Stony, where the familiar and the strange are joined:
                                                            tangential
Marriages.
                        Imprisoned in the tall towers time kindles a ringing
Of iron bells
                        Iron round
                                    bronze round
Resounding gongs clang in the nineteen tongues of the town
And the burnished sounds of the hours of dawn downsail and sing
Into the shadowy strees . . .
                                    nightwater
                                                timesbourne . . .
                                                                    Where we
Daily are borne, and dally our days along and sadly and gayly
Light up our candles in search of our hourly bread.

And now, putting off its suit of lights, its electric mythologies,
The platonic city floats up out of the dark:
                                                    insubstantial
Structures, framework of dream and nightmare, a honeyed static
Incorporeal which the light condenses. A thin dust,
The fictions of time and custom, is clothing its mineral bones;

Out of the vapors of rent and habit the walls regain
Their untransparent strength; an ectoplasm of sweat and money
Crystallizes into roofs and docks; the bells collect
Around their bronze and song the cages of shimmering towers
And the footsteps of early workers are building the streets to the river.

✦ IN EARLY AUTUMN

On a day when the trees are exchanging the cured gold of the sun,
And the heavy oils of darkness in the rivers of their circular hearts
thicken;
   when desperation has entered the song of the locust;
   When, in abandoned farmsites, the dark stays longer
   In the closed parlor;
       a day when exhausted back-country roads,
Those barges loaded with sunlight and the bodies of dead animals,
Disappear into the Sand Hills under a swollen sun;
A day, too, when the sizzling flies are fingering their rosaries of blood
In the furry cathedrals of spent flesh, the left-over
Gone-green goners from the golden summer —

THEN I know a place with three dead dogs and two dead deer in one ditch.
I feel the displacement of minerals,
The stone grown fossils,
Under this hill of bones that calls my flesh its home.

✦ THE RESTLESS NIGHT

Oh God help me now to cry out and bear witness;
Help me to send forth a great cry at the darkness;
Help me to waken my brother from his dream of rage and fire;
Help me to cry out in defence of my brother.
      Hush; do not let a moment's delirium
      Negate the decorum of a lifetime of indifference.
      If you should cry out there would be nothing to say.
      Hush; you would only waken the others.

Oh who among the bright hosts of the heavenly angels
Will call forward my name on a dark day?
Unless I cry forth to point my dark to the light,
To speak for my brother, that day who will call my name?
      Hush; do not let the temporary fever
      Astound the moment with its population of phantoms.
      You do not wish to appear ridiculous.
      Hush; there is really nothing you could say.

Oh if I do not rouse him who will awaken my brother
Dozing in this enduring instant of eternal damnation?
Sleepwalking in his immortality which is only lifelong –
Oh Watcher, help me to cry forth to my brother.
      Hush; do not let the guilt of a dark hour
      Breed the excess of revolutionary sympathy.
      Do not trust anguish; it is without function.
      Hush; the day comes: wherein no man speaks.

◆ AFTERNOON OF A McGRATH

For my son Tomasito McGrath
after a visit to McGrath, Minnesota
(Aitken County)
early winter '74-'75

This morning there was one McGrath in Aitken County.
                                                        Now
There are three: the town, Tomasito, and myself.
                                        And at this rate of growth
The County will remain alive at least ten minutes longer,
Though the town is disappearing: fast: in a thickening snow:
Which is also the snow of time, the secret invisible snow
That falls in summer and falls in the fall and in spring: the snow
We are all disappearing into – all but Tomasito
Who has found a god-dog to mush home with if he knew where that was.

This town, which carries our name into the rising night,
Is one of those lost places in which I have found myself
Often . . . though they always had other names – and sometimes I did.
What could I expect to find in a place where the lakes hold only
Private water? A walk or a wake away from the Dead
Sea of Mille Lacs where all class-struggle is ethnic?
                                                        Place
Where each grave plot is bespoke and the loudest talk is on tombstones?
Did I think to push open a gate and enter a century of sleep
Where only myself is awake? But that's just the world I live in
Outside the township limits . . .
                                    Perhaps I expected to find
Death McGrath, that stranger I meet so often in dreams,
The one I thought was myself disguised in the drag of death?
Perhaps he is one of these Indians, now in full retreat
(With their white comrades) from the shots and the double shots of General
Alcohol?
                    But it's not the bargirl, inside whose head
It is snowing, as it snows in mine, and behind whose eyes I see
The slow turn to the left of those permanent low-pressure systems . . .

96

And that's McGrath. I will never forget it, now, Tomasito –
Our ghosts are here forever now because you were here
With this snow and this bar and that dog – see: what you have invented!
And so I will put this poem under a stone somewhere
On a road I will never walk on again, as I have done
Another time.
     Or put it with our hidden wishing stone
To remember us by "forever": now: as the town disappears
Into the blizzard . . .
     and all the McGraths drift into
That snow, that permanent white where all our colors fade.

The night is closing down. But I'd like McGrath to continue
Beyond this winter and those to come – though THAT beyond
Is beyond all hope.
    So let me stop: here: then . . .
          – drifting
Into the universe and past all stars: toward those
Dark holes in space I must recognize as home.

✦ THE DREAM RANGE

1.

When, young, I slept in a cold bed
My sleep was classical and calm.
The fallow field, the prunéd vine
The call of curlew and of kine –
These claimed and tuned my pastoral head:
I had no need for the dream range.

2.

My wife was softig and baroque,
But kept a hard board in the bed.
The burning colors of her day,
Eclipsing darkness cooled away.
Still, all that dark till I awoke,
I had the run of the dream range.

3.

From a dream of existential honey
I woke to voices crying *"more!"* –
Downpayments to save the nuptial manse
(From the fell clutch of low finance)
And gadgets might shame a metal whore –
And *that* was life on the dream range.

4.

Then Law came, like a walking turd,
Faith, Hope and Charity to divorce.
She kept the board, she kept the bed,
She kept the coldness in her head.
I paid for every loving word – O,
To hell! with life on the dream range!

◆ THE END OF THE WORLD

The end of the world: it was given to me to see it.
Came in the black dark, a bulge in the starless sky,
A trembling at the heart of the night, a twitching of the webby flesh
       of the earth.
And out of the bowels of the street one beastly, ungovernable cry.

Came and I recognized it: the end of the world.
And waited for the lightless plunge, the fury splitting the rock.
And waited: a kissing of leaves: a whisper of man-killing ancestral night –
Then: a tinkle of music, laughter from the next block.

Yet waited still: for the awful traditional fire,
Hearing mute thunder, the long collapse of sky.
It falls forever. But no one noticed. The end of the world provoked
Out of the dark a single and melancholy sigh

From my neighbor who sat on his porch drinking beer in the dark.
No: I was not God's prophet. Armageddon was never
And always: this night in a poor street where a careless irreverent laughter
Postpones the end of the world: in which we live forever.

◆ THE BREAD OF THIS WORLD; PRAISES III

On the Christmaswhite plains of the floured and flowering kitchen table
The holy loaves of the bread are slowly being born:
Rising like low hills in the steepled pastures of light –
Lifting the prairie farmhouse afternoon on their arching backs.

It must be Friday, the bread tells us as it climbs
Out of itself like a poor man climbing up on a cross
Toward transfiguration.
                            And it is a Mystery, surely,
If we think that this bread rises only out of the enigma
That leavens the Apocalypse of yeast, or ascends on the beards and beads
Of a rosary and priesthood of barley those Friday heavens
Lofting . . .

                    But we who will eat the bread when we come in
Out of the cold and dark know it is a deeper mystery
That brings the bread to rise:
                                    it is the love and faith
Of large and lonely women, moving like floury clouds
In farmhouse kitchens, that rounds the loaves and the lives
Of those around them . . .
                            just as we know it is hunger –
Our own and others' – that gives all salt and savor to bread.

But that is a workaday story and this is the end of the week.

◆ POEM — UNFINISHED POEM

What a way to spend the golden years, Tomasito!
Jackassing around in all weather, pickheaded and spade handed,
(Never closer to ten-strike than the Mother-in-Law Lode!)
Through deserts temporal and spiritual where every badlands bonanza
Turns into borrasca . . . and always trying to find the handle
For the Malpais: the name for the As-Yet-Undiscovered Country,
And find the Logos and Lost Dutchman of the One and Ore-bearing Word . . .
Many cold camps on the trail of live language, little cheechaco,
And my only companion a burro who brays like a bourgeois poet!

A whole week wasted: packing through one black pass!
And another morning gone crossing the rotten talus
To con the quartz of a cliff-face, then over the ridge
And into a new river-system – the rock barren and rotten,
Snow on the breakneck slope and ice right down to the water . . .

And all in the vain search for a single word, and one
That's probably full of fool's gold at that!
Damn crazy way to spend so much of a life –
To hell with that word, Tomasito! Let's go out in the sun!

✦ WHEN WE SAY GOODBYE

It is not because we are going –
Though the sea may begin at the doorstep, though the highway
May already have come to rest in our front rooms . . .

It is because, beyond distance, or enterprise
And beyond the lies and surprises of the wide and various worlds,
Beyond the flower and the bird and the little boy with his large questions
We notice our shadows:
Going . . .
– slowly, but going,
In slightly different directions –
Their speeds increasing –
Growing shorter, shorter
As we enter the intolerable sunlight that never grows old or kind.

✦ POEM

How could I have come so far?
(And always on such dark trails!)
I must have travelled by the light
Shining from the faces of all those I have loved.

✦ YOU TAUGHT ME

All those years, alone,
Married to the intense uninteresting life . . .
And, until you came, Tomasito,
I didn't even know my name!

✦ POEM

When I carry my little son in the cold
I begin to turn into a hollow tree:
I want to carry him more deeply,
Inside the warmth of my heart.

✦ THE CHANGELING

Squatting, serious,
His small hand locked on my middle finger,
He digs a shallow hole in the earth, buries
His "wishing stone," covers it up,
Forgets it, maybe.

What will he find if he ever comes back to this place?
He is older
Coarser perhaps his hands already
Hardened from holding a gun maybe from stroking the wrong women

From labor and money.

If he remembers this place the secret
Place he has hidden his luck, by the blasted tree by the hidden
Pool, by the rock, by the river, in the hollow hill of a cave

— Whatever he finds, it will be his no longer.
These little boys can never, never return.

✦ POEM

My little son, laughing, singing . . .
Why these tears
trembling at my eyes?

◆ THE ORPHAN

It has been a long time
Since he was a little boy.
And in all those years
— no one with whom he could cry.

◆ THE ENEMY

He is there, somewhere . . .
                    high up over the pass
We must travel
            in air thinner than spirit,
Bloodless,
         structure of cold fog. His rifle
Gleams.
       He waits as we cross the ridge.

Son, you will see him
Sometimes:
          at the foot of the bed,
                   grieving,
A wavering presence in your fever-dream.
Or seeming to grieve.
            Wearing the mask of your father.

◆ CELEBRATION

How wonderful, Tomasito!
All of us here!
Together . . .
A little while
On the road through . . .

✦ ORDONNANCE

During a war the poets turn to war
In praise of the merit of the death of the ball-turret gunner.
It is well arranged: each in his best manner
One bleeds, one blots — as they say, it has happened before.

After a war, who has news for the poet?
If sunrise is Easter, noon is his winey tree.
Evening arrives like a postcard from his true country
And the seasons shine and sing. Each has its note

In the song of the man in his room in his house in his head remembering
The ancient airs. It is good. But is it good
That he should rise once to his song on the fumes of blood
As a ghost to his meat? Should rise so, once, in anger

And then no more? Now the footsteps ring on the stone —
The Lost Man of the century is coming home from his work.
"They are fighting, fighting" — Oh, yes. But somewhere else. In the dark.
The poet reads by firelight as the nations burn.

✦ ALL THE DEAD SOLDIERS

In the chill rains of the early winter I hear something –
A puling anger, a cold wind stiffened by flying bone –
Out of the north . . .
                       and remember, then, what's up there:
That ghost-bank: home: Amchitka: boot hill. . . .

They must be very tired, those ghosts; no flesh sustains them
And the bones rust in the rain.
                           Reluctant to go into the earth
The skulls gleam: wet; the dog-tag forgets the name;
The statistics (wherein they were young) like their crosses, are weathering out.

They must be very tired.
                   But I see them riding home,
Nightly: crying weak lust and rage: to stand in the dark,
Forlorn in known rooms, unheard near familiar beds:
Where lie the aging women: who were so lovely: once.

✦ LAMENT FOR PABLO NERUDA

We may well ask now: "Where are the lilacs?" Yes . . .
And where now are the "metaphysics covered with poppies?"

There are vertical streets in Chile that end in the mankilling sea.
Up these the salt is climbing like a mineral snake on the stairs
Made from the bones of dead men. There are dead men too in the plaza,
Under the salt of the moon where traitorous generals sit
Sipping the wine of silence and crossing out names on a page . . .

You have seen the dead in the square, Neruda, and you have known
Those wounded lands where the poor are dying against the walls
In the shadow of Administrations, in the shadow of Law, in the hollow
Ministries where workers are murdered by the mere echoes of money
And miners are abandoned in the black galleries.

                                    But hope is not lost
For you also saw the International Brigade as it entered Madrid:
"The thin and hard and ripe and ardent brigade of stone."
I want to believe you, Neruda, old Commissar of roses!
I hear your furious ghost calling in the midnight streets!
I see your generous blood staining the dollar bills!

And I long for the angry angel to rise over Machu Picchu,
For the guerilla entering the plaza where defeated generals wait.

♦ A NOTE ON THE LATE ELECTIONS

Behold, Friends, once more the Revolution has performed its famous
Disappearing act! And never before has one been preceded
By so many prophets! By so many holy books – all in translation!
By so many young men with long hair, so many poets with short
Breath!
      AND the elephant bells!
              Oo la! And incense.
                       And

The flowers!
        The flowers, alas, which never found the barrel
Of the gun that power grows out of.
              And now the President, reborn
Out of the mystical body of the One and Universal
Voting machine, takes off the mask.
            A thick and heavy
Darkness, like rust, is collecting in the amplified guitars.
The President with make the Airplane fly! He will make the Grateful Dead
Truly grateful! The President is casting the *other* I Ching. . . .

A hard rain is falling; the roads are icing up.
But in every drop of the rain the sailors of the Potemkin wake. . . .

✦ THE END OF THE LINE

The Iron Horse is rusting,
In the statue-fenced plazas of the nameless towns,
Who once crossed the wild prairies, cursing,
(Voice of feathers and smoke)
In his carbon rages, on his whirling shoes.

The mourning dove inherits his ancient voice;
But who will awaken the heroic sleeper out of his history –
That iron road to Noplace where he lately arrived
In a gunfire of oratory near where the soldiers lie?

Alas! Joe Hill, the millionaires have thrown your torch backward
              into this future!
Where now the locomotive is burning among the patriots.
Fourth of July. Hot . . .
      Daddy, what's at the end of the line?
      Baby, I tell you, the big train don't go there no more.

✦ POEM

You out there, so secret.
What makes you think you're alone?

✦ THE NEED FOR DICTIONARIES II

What is named
Is known.
By its disguises.

✦ POEM

In the list of one thousand false addresses
Why do I find the town
Where my true love was born?

✦ WHAT WE THINK WE KNOW

Apple blossom and
      squirrel
           on the same bough

And the late wet snow of spring.

✦ FOR A CRITIC WHO TRIES TO WRITE POEMS

Well, well, little poet!
Still looking for a dew drop
In the middle of a thunderstorm!

◆ REVISIONIST POEM: MACHADO

Poor and desperate men
Invented four things that are useful at sea:
Sails, rudders, oars
And the fear of drowning

◆ POEM

Light flares from the tombstones. . . .
Cemeteries *ought* to be sunny –
So many graves here
You'd think we had buried
All our darkness.

◆ REVISIONIST POEM – OCTAVIO PAZ

The world is an invention of the spirit the spirit
Is an invention of the body the body
Is an invention of the world

◆ PARABLE

Anonymity has a name;
Which Terror knows.

✦ THREE FUNCTIONS OF IRONY

1. The shield
2. The carapace
3. The ambush

✦ POEM

Down the small and crooked road
I walk straight toward my death.
How marvelous the moon sits on my shoulder!
The wind is laughing as I laugh.

✦ POEM

The long wound of the summer –
Stitched
by cicadas.

✦ PARABLE

The stick of the blind man
Invents a new darkness.

✦ THE NEWS AND THE WEATHER

Serene night cold November
Full moon the neighbors
Quarrelling hair greyer almost
Sixty

✦ ANOTHER SEASON

Fall work almost done . . .
Plowing finished and now only
The butchering still to do.

All summer, from the distant house, I heard
A slow grindstone, singing,
Where someone was sharpening the knives.

✦ POEM

Through the fog
The gulls
Carry the sea
Inland

✦ REMEMBERING LOVES AND DEATHS

They happened in us . . .
But later we moved away –
Or they did.

Went west.
Went south to the goldfields.
Disappeared somewhere beyond Salt Lake or Denver –
Their roads are still in the map of our flesh:
Easy to get to almost any time
Around midnight.

But the land shifts and changes, the map
Gets out of date,
The century stretches its joints,
And one day we stand by the marked tree and ask: WAS IT HERE
WAS IT HERE
While, stunned but tireless,
Memory, the lodestone that always points toward pain,
Hunts, slow and sluggish for its North,
Turning through the thickening crystals of tired flesh
That was pure honey, once.

✦ A THEORY

As Thucydides said,
What is history?
Greeks!
Murdering
Greeks

✦ THE WORLD; THE LOVERS; FALLING STARS

for Alice

Peaked in an immortal flame
The mortal moth-like lovers burn.
The love that sets their limbs alight
(Searing the snow of breast and thigh)
Can have no history but to die,
Yet cannot change. Across the night
Radiance of falling stars is borne:
Impermanent. These are the same
Who burn in the contradictions of
The strict and sensual laws of love.

Passing a point of no return,
An age consumed in instant flame,
The lovers cannot save themselves.
Bound in a swift triumphant arc,
Like falling stars, they light the dark
And loveless world. From private hells
All common daily good is torn,
Without history or name
Almost: though brilliance in the air
Lingers when a star was there.

✦ FROM A LONG WAY OUT OF PAH-GATZIN-KAY

With all those I love
Shining
In radiant light
On the other side of the world,
I lie down in this
Darkness.
I straighten my legs.
I close my eyes.
I try to dream of my own waking.
I hold myself in my own arms like a dead friend.

✦ DON'T THINK YOU KNOW MY NAME!

And so I am getting old!
Like a tree in the forest
I am shedding branches and leaves, and around my feet
Are enough dry twigs for three English martyrs –
And every son-of-a-bitch wants to set me on fire. . . .

Not important of course. I'll have to walk out in the snow
In any case. Where else is there to turn?
So if you see me coming, a man made out of ice,
Splintering light like rainbows at every crazed joint of my body,
Better get out of the way: this black blood won't burn
And the fierce acids of winter are smoking in this cold heart.

✦ POEM

My little son comes running with open arms!
Sometimes I can't bear it,
Father.
Did I, too,
Open your heart almost to breaking?

✦ EVERYTHING IN ORDER

I'll never get to where I'm going!
No surprise in that . . .
Plugging through this deep snow,
My arms heavy with the weight of the dead . . .

✦ NIGHT WORK

It's too much: this hard work –
All night chipping on the stone of sleep . . .

And then to wake in the morning
And find only the old, known,
Statue of solitude –
Hardly changed at all . . .

✦ TRIUMPHAL MARCH

After the long strike
We continued walking in circles
For a long time: dreaming:
Many nights many days
Dizzy (but not with success)
From the round dance of our struggle!

O Solidarity!
What did it matter we'd lost?

◆ THE RETURN

The trees are never the same
                            twice
                                    the animals
                                                  the birds or
The little river lying on its back in the sun or the sun or
The varying moon changing over the changing hills
Constant.
                  It is this, still, that most I love about them.

I enter by dark or day:
                            that green noise, dying
Alive and living its death, that inhuman circular singing,
May call me stranger . . .
                            Or the little doors of the bark open
And I enter that other home outside the tent of my skin . . .

On such days, on such midnights, I have gone, I will go,
Past the human, past the animal, past the bird,
To the old mothers who stand with their feet in the loamy dark
And their green and gold praises playing into the sun . . .

For a little while, only. (It is a long way back.)
But at least, and if but for a moment, I have almost entered the stone.
Then fear and love call. I am cast out. Alien,
On the bridge of fur and of feather I go back to the world I have known.

from

✦ **ECHOES INSIDE THE LABYRINTH** ✦

Once, when the grand nudes, golden as fields of grain –
But touched with a rose flush like homeric cliches of dawn! –
Dreamed in prudential calm above the parochial lightning
Of bad whiskey;
            and when the contentious and turbulent General,
Handcrafted of fringed buckskin, legend, aromatic gunsmoke,
On the Greasygrass Little Bighorn lay down his long blond hair
At last at peace
          in his quiet kingdom
                 over the back-bar:
Then: the myth of Beer was born and the continental thirst!

O Beer we praise thee and honor thy apostolic ways!
Primero: for the glory of thy simple and earthy ancestors! As:
Instance: the noble Barley, its hairy and patriarchal
Vigor: golden
          in the windy lagers of manfarmed machine-framed fields;
Or in shocks or stooks
       tented
         like Biblical tribes
            bearded
(But without the badrap of their barbaric god) gay,
Insouciant as encampments of the old Oglalla Sioux
Where each lodge opens eastward to the Land of the Morning Sun!

Praise for:
      segundo: the lacy and feminine elegance of the hops
Raising into the sun their herbal essence, medicinal,
Of the scent of the righttime rain fallen on rich earth.
They lift their tiny skirts – of Linnean Latin made!
Like those great nudes of the barrooms: souls of the newborn beer!

And we praise also Yeast: the tireless marine motors
Of its enigmatic enzymes, and its esters: like the submarine stars
Of astral rivers and horoscopic estuaries shining.

And we praise, last, the secret virtue of pure water,
A high lord among the Five Elements, gift of the heavens,
Its mineral integrity and the savor of secret iron!

Guitars are distilled from wine: from the politics of moonlight,
From the disasters of tequila and the edible worm in the deep well
Of mescal.
                    But from beer comes banjos and jazz bands ecstatic
Trumpets midnight Chicago early thirties Bix.

It was Beer that invented Sunday from the long and salty days
Of the workday week:
                              that from the fast beer on horseback or the warm
Beer of the burning fields of the harvest, when the barley comes in,
Fermented the sabbatarian leisure;
                              that, in the eye of the workstorm,
For the assemblyline robotniki and the miner who all week long
Must cool his thirst at the root of the dark flower of the coal
Offered reprieve;
                    and for slow men on tractors (overalled
And perpetually horny) turned off their motors for the Sabbath calm.

It is farther from Sunday to Monday than to any other day of the week.
And Monday begins farther from home than a month of Sundays.
It begins in a deeper darkness than other days, and comes
From farther away, but swifter, to the sounds of alarums and whistles.
Six hours ahead of the sun it appears: first in dreams
Where we shudder, smelling the strength of sweat from the earlier east,
(Already at hard labor) and our sleep is filling with fireflies
From ancient forges, the hot sparks flying; then
It appears as grief for a lost world: that round song and commune
When work was a handclasp – before it built fences around us.

Monday is a thief: he carries in his weak and tiny fist
A wilted flower wrenched from our Sunday garden . . . still blue
With hope: but fast fading in the heat of his metal grasp.

Tuesday is born and borne like an old horse, coming
Home to the stall from the salt of the harvest fields, where, hitched
To sun and stubble, flyplagued and harness galled, sweatcrusted,
(The lather from under his collar whitening the martingales)
Teamed up he lugged the stammering machines through the twenty
                    one-mile rounds
On the slowly narrowing field . . .

Tuesday comes without flowers –
Neither Queen Anne's lace nor even Yarrow or Golden Rod –
(Most colorless of all the days of our week and work)
                                        without thunder,
(Like the old horse too tired to roll in the dust)
                                    without even
The anguish of Monday exile. It follows us home from our work.

Wednesday is born in the midweek waste like the High Sierra
Rising out of the desert, Continental Divide
In the long division of the septimal and sennight thirst;
                                        from where,
At Bridger's Pass or near Pike's Peak, at the last pine,
Cold, in the Wednesday snow, we halt for a moment and see:
Faraway, shining, the saltwhite glow of that Promised Land:
The Coast of Sunday –
                gold and maltgold –
                        beyond Thursday's Mohave heat.

But Thursday is born in that mid-point halt at the hinge of the week
Where we seem too tired to push open the ancient five-barred gate
That lets on flowery holts and heaths and the faraway antic hay
Where leisure sprawls and dances in the fair of work-free fun . . .
Here thirst compounds his salty rectitudes: in Skinny Thursday:
That midweek Dog Day curse in Monday's cast-off shoes!

Friday is born in desperation, in the shadow of parables,
In the tent of Surplus Value, in the hot breath of Profit.
Yet it cometh forth as a fawn, yea as a young lamb
It danceth on prophetic mountains whose feet the Jordan laves!
Here is the time of the Dream Drinking, where our loves and needs
Come under the same roof-tree.
                        Evening of hope.
                                Freer
Than manic Saturday and more adventurous than Sunday's calm.
Now we cast lots for our workweek clouts or put them in pawn!
And the night opens its enormous book wherein we invent our lives . . .

Saturday's children had far to go. We arrive as strangers
Entering the Indian Nation in the paycheck's prairie schooner,
Homesteaders in the last free land of the West . . .

Already

The Sooners, those Johnny-Come-Earlies and claim jumpers
On the choicest barstools assert their squatter's rights . . .
They claim (these Dream Drinkers) – 40 acres and a mule
Or a King Ranch bigger than all of Texas!

It is Time they would

Reclaim from the burntout wagon train of the workweek waste.
Here each is Prince in his Castle Keep, but, outside, Time
Elaborates warp and woof and the ancient Enemies gather . . .
O blessed Beer, old Equalizer – doom for Comanches:
Shot down on Saturday's mesa in the flash of a 6 pack of Schlitz!

Deadflower, harness, halt-in-the-snow, dogday, holy hour!
By these five signs and passages we knew the laboring week
As we traveled and travailled toward Castle Keep, Compañeros Trabajeros!
And now, where Sundays buzz like flies caught in a web,
Drained of their workday strength, the golden spirit of Beer
Comes to lead us out of the net, if only a moment,
To where Possibility rolls out its secret roads
To picnic places where Potato Salad and the Olive and the Onion
And Ham-and-Cheese sandwiches position the kids on the grass;
Or to lazy creeks or lakes where the lunkers lounge and lunge,
Guides us;

or into the popcorn smell and afternoon rituals

Of baseball fields shills us:

where forever the high homer,

Smoking, of the great stars, writes their names on the sky . . .
And later, the firefly-lighted evenings, on back porches –
The vegetable lightning of those small stars caught in the grass . . .

Beer, birra, la bière, tiswin, pivo, cerveza –
In all its names and forms, like a polymorphic god, praise!
As, among Mexican stars and guitars: *Cresta Blanca*
And *Cuautemoc*: to be drunk under Popocatépetl
And Xochimilco;

and *Fix*

(named for Fuchs) in Greece,

Either in Ammonia Square where the poor go or in Syntagma
Where the umbrellas gather the bourgeoisie in their shade;
And *San Miguel* where the Philippines offer expendable chickens;
And *Heineken* cold as the Hans Brinker canals where the Dutch
Are skating around on tulips and wooden shoes; and *Pilsener*
Resurrected from Nazi and allied bombings, old-world gold,
Of the Czechs and Slavs;
                                and all the melodious beers of Spain;
And of England, land of the mild and bitter: *O'Keefe's* and *Watney's Ales*;
And, of Ireland, *Guinness Stout* with its arms of turf and gunfire;
And Australia's *Melbourne Bitter* from way down under!

Beer which passes through vats like the multiple stomachs of ruminants
To be lagered in sunken cloisters in monkish gloom till the day
When, on the brewery dray, it is ceremonially borne
Through the sunny morning towns by those great and noble beasts
Those horses with necks of thunder and fetlocks like hairy paint brushes.

Beer of Milwaukee! Beer of St. Louis! Where Lewis and Clark
Passed in the days of the fur trade and the wide ranging voyageurs.
And pass still, like ghosts, day after day, unseen
And forgotten: still hunting that West that was lost as soon as found –
Legends in search of a legend:
                                As the new beers of the West
Lucky and *Lone Star*, *Olympia*, *Grain Belt*, *Coors*
Seek the phantom perfection of the mythic beers of the past!

Beer, not to be sipped but lifted against the palate –
Like the mystical cargo of argosies: lofted into the holds
Where the hideaway ports of the Spanish Main set their top-gallants
To drag their island-anchors into the New World!

Comestible beer that puts the hop in the Welsh Rabbit!
Beer-soup-du-jour that causes the cheese to sing!
Beer that transmogrifies the evening's peasant pot roast!
That metamorphizes the onion in the Sunday carbonade!

Praise, then, for *pulque* and *kvass*, for *chang*, for *weissbier*
For *suk* and *sonshu*, for *bousa* and all the hand-me-down
Home brews!
                              No firewater, aqua forte, blast-head or forty-rod
But heart medicine: made for fast days or fiesta:
For the worker in his vestments of salt at the end of our laboring days,
Or for corroboree and ceilidh where the poem sings and says:
Praise for the golden liquor of Wakan Tanka or god!
Praise for its holy office – O offer hosanna and laud!
By sip, by sup, by tot, by tipple, by chuglug – *all* ways:
Hallelujah! For the People's Beer! And for all His comrades: praise!

✦ WINTER ROADS

In the spring thaw
The winter roads over the cold fields
Disappear
In front of the last sled.

All summer they sleep
Hidden and forgot
Under the green sea of the wheat.

Now, in autumn,
They rise
Suddenly
Out of the golden stubble.
They arch their backs in the sun
And move slow and crooked across the fields
Looking for winter.

✦ BEYOND THE RED RIVER

The birds have flown their summer skies to the south,
And the flower-money is drying in the banks of bent grass
Which the bumble bee has abandoned. We wait for a winter lion,
Body of ice-crystals and sombrero of dead leaves.

A month ago, from the salt engines of the sea,
A machinery of early storms rolled toward the holiday houses
Where summer still dozed in the pool-side chairs, sipping
An aging whiskey of distances and departures.

Now the long freight of autumn goes smoking out of the land.
My possibles are all packed up, but still I do not leave.
I am happy enough here, where Dakota drifts wild in the universe,
Where the prairie is starting to shake in the surf of the winter dark.

◆ HISTORY

All night the wind
Yelled at the house,
The trees squeaked and hushed
But the wind would not.
All night the trees complained
And the rain rushed and rained.

Now in the cool
Morning the trees stand, tall,
Still and all composed –
Sun on their sunny pages.
Of the storm only the riled
Creek remembers; and rages.

✦ AUTUMN SONG

Autumn has emptied heaven of its birds
And stretched a silence on the loud sea.
Gone is the last leaf and the last flower,
And all the gauds of summer are undone.

> Winter cuts off our feet. But we must dance
> In Spring's conspiracy of circumstance:
> Swallows sickling air's invisible grass
> Sketch hieroglyphs that translate at a glance
> To greenest meaning.
>   The sun, love's looking-glass,
> Summer, that stokes the furnace of the bee,
> Honey all nature in one grand romance –
> The ambience of consanguinity
> Hurls its huge myth around the world at me.

But now the sports and sunny shows are done.
A deadflower clock ticks out a year of seed.
The season's losses hide the summer road,
And crows talk hoarsely in the frozen wood.

◆ THE DREAMS OF WILD HORSES

Night and full moon.
A profane rhythm of
Man-throwing unsanctified broncos
Stampedes like wildfire
Into the sin-colored badlands.

Here, nightlong they invent new names,
Christening themselves
In the cold creek.
The dawn sky expels
Their lunar voices.

Harnessed to sunlight,
Sowing the city of silence,
They plant their names
In the dark.

Crazy Horse is dead.
Parched buffalo bones.
Moonlight weathering in the dry corn.

◆ GO ASK THE DEAD

1.

The soldier, past full retreat, is marching out of the grave
As he lies under dying grass in the slow judgment of time
On which he has lost his grasp.
                                    And lost his taste as well –
For, tell-tale as fast as it will, no tongue can put salt on his name.
The captain sun has done with this numberless underground.

2.

He has seeded out of that flesh where the flashing lights first fade
In the furry sky of the head.
                                    And the orient admiral brain
Has seen its images go like ensigns blown from a line –
Those raving signals.
                        All quality's bled from his light,
And number (he's all thumbs now) divides where infinities fail.

3.

Grand winds of the sky might claim; or the blue hold
Of ocean accept;
                    or fire sublime –
                                    though it's earth
Now hinders and halters
                        him.
                                    But those underground birds, his bones,
(Homeless all havens save here) fly out of their low-hilled heavens
And shine up into the light to blaze in his land's long lie.

4.

And long they lie there but not for love in the windy contentions
Of sun and rain, shining. This endless invasion of death
Darkens our world. There is no argument that will move them.
"You are eating our light!" they cry. "Where have you taken the sun?
You have climbed to the moon on a ladder of dead men's bones!"

✦ FRESCO: DEPARTURE FOR
AN IMPERIALIST WAR

They stand there weeping in the stained daylight.
Nothing can stop them now from reaching the end of their youth.

Somewhere the Mayor salutes a winning team.
Somewhere the diplomats kiss in the long corridors of history.

Somewhere a politician is grafting a speech
On the green tree of American money.

Somewhere prayer; somewhere orders and papers.
Somewhere the poor are gathering illegal arms.

Meanwhile they are there on that very platform.
The train sails silently toward them out of American sleep,

And at last the two are arrived at the very point of departure.
He goes toward death and she toward loneliness.

Weeping, their arms embrace the only country they love.

◆ REMEMBERING THE
CHILDREN OF AUSCHWITZ

We know the story. The children
Are lost in the deep forest –
Though it is the same forest
In which we all are born.

But somehow it has changed:
A new kind of darkness,
Or something they never noticed,
Has colored the pines and the larches.

And now appears the Bird,
(Bird of a strange dreaming)
To lead them, as tales foretold,
Over the little streams

Into the garden of order
Where trees no longer menaced,
And a little house was protected
Inside its candy fences.

And all seemed perfectly proper:
The little house was covered
with barbwire and marzipan;
And the Witch was there; and the Oven.

Perhaps they never noticed –
After all that disorder
Of being lost – that they'd come
To the Place named in the stories.

Perhaps there was even peace –
A little – after disorder,
Before they awoke into
A dream of deeper horror.

And now the Bird will never
Take them across the river
(Though they knew how to walk on water).
They become part of the weather.

They have become the Ascensions.
When we lift up our eyes,
In any light, we see them:
Darkening all our skies.

✦ THE POET OF THE PRISON ISLE:
RITSOS AGAINST THE COLONELS

for Carolyn Forché

So there you are,
Jannis Ritsos,
On that island of pure salt
Where it only rains on the dead.

*   *   *

Statues of sand statutes
Of gall
Enormous legends of the Platonic Republic founded on gunpowder.

Hush
The Colonels are coming
The King is Coming
Tra La

*   *   *

Meanwhile you are dying. And harder than in any poem.
Of course we are all trying to keep the frontiers open people are doing des-
    perate things to save you some people read the times and are indignant
    some people read the past and are indignant some madwoman is read-
    ing her personal memoirs personally over WEVD explaining the values
    of those who put you out there the first time.
All's ordnung as Ez sez and let's not forget the poets carefully writing in
    lowercase and erasing if they hit a capital.

*   *   *

Well, there are damn few capitols where they might want you
Outside the revolutionary world.
I guess
The poets and all being what they are you'll die where you're at.
A sad thing
Because you are the only one in the world who heard
Those terrible trains in the heads of widows
The trains that carry the conscripts
To that bosses' war – the one
Just over the border.

✦ IN THE SLEEP OF REASON

The pilot, returned, sees the village
Unwrap itself
                in slow motion
Releasing its nameless people into history,
On film.

        But he is still up there,
Dreaming,
With his toy gun
Lying in the high grass
At 40,000 feet.

◆ USES OF THE LOST POETS

for Don Gordon

The poems of others he clipped and saved in those distant summers –
No farther from him than himself – have faded into the dark,
Almost . . . the dew that died on the dry page weathering away –
Out of its image – to climb the ladder of sun and wind
To the cradling sea gathered; and the metaphorical diamond,
That once worked names on glass, gone back to the soft country
Of carbon, memory, letters . . .
                                        to the wounds of the bituminous man.

Child of fancy, what did you hope from those distant voices
Crying immortal anguish in the fallen world of your desk
Abandoned, now? Oh, the boy was only trying
To climb on the dewy stairs of the poem his contemporary built
Toward the sound of a friend, perhaps, or the name cut into glass, some . . .
Thing to hold more permanent than a flower pressed in a book –
If the firefly is summer, the poem *might* be the star of time.

A century of cicadas has burnt holes in those paper heavens
In the few breaths that he drew while the poems lay curled in sleep,
In his grave notebook saved – gone into time like smoke
With the winking generations of the firefly, the dew, the impermanent
Diamond . . .
                        And now he must fly his own kite in the dark of the moon
To gather what lightning may lead him dangerously out of that dark
And up the homing stairway to set a light on his desk.

For he is no boy, now, but himself the bituminous man:
Burning: and not to be diamond but for usefulness of that light –
His own – for others: the wink and bite of international
Code to guide or home on for those on blind ways: to save
(Now that stars fall, the zodiac shifts and the lodestar drifts and lies)
Or hope to save (from loss and terror of these times)
To save the lonesome traveller lost on the nightbound roads.

✦ PASSAGES

for Tomasito

They come in in tiny boats . . .
                              come out of nowhere.
And the boats are of heavy stone:
                              basalt . . .
                                    slate . . .
                                          dark
And clumsy – like old watering troughs furry with moss
(And the horses that drank of that water are long long dead).

                                          Down there –
Where the boats come in down the long roads through the limestone –
I searched for you everywhere, wading through the heavy light,
Scaly, where it seeps down through the slate . . .
                              loaded with darkness
Like the leaffall from stone trees in a heavy autumn of stone.

The leaves of those slate trees falling in that tired and heavy light
Are clouding my eyes now . . .
                              as I remember.
                              Down there
Where the soul boats drift: down: slow: in the dark
Mineralized water of the underworld rivers I called your name . . .

Topaz, jasper, sardonyx, carnelian, turquoise, aquamarine –
The hours of stone.
                    Granite, limestone, sandstone, marble –
The seasons.
              Through that fatal weather, oh Friend and Stranger –
You: reading the crystal of this page! – it was you I sought!

              *   *   *

                                          Down there
I searched for others: to set them free: in the backwoods of granite,
In the underground of obsidian, among the anomalous layers
And blind intrusions (basalt dikes cutting conformable strata
Where the class struggle faltered) *there* I sought the Hero . . .

Travertine of hidden springs . . .

                                                  terminal granite

                                                                   and the black

Of the primal preterite: I passed through them like secret water –
Like a mineral wind through those stony heavens whose rain falls
As beads of turquoise, and thunder is a distant sigh of rock . . .

Nothing.

                This rumor of class war from the upper world of the streets
Where my comrades fought in the winter of money – that only.

                                                              The Hero:

You: Reader: whose fate was to free the Bound Woman for the vernal
Rising and revolution on the promised springtime earth –

                                                            nowhere.

. . . Slum, souk, casbah, ghetto, the transform faults
Of industrial parks – I worked these stony limits.

                                                      On the killing wall,
Scored by the firing squads, I chalked our rebel terms.
I drank the mephitic waters and made my bed in the dark.

                *   *   *

It was then – in my need and blind search, in the nightrock, faltering,
As I slowly changed into stone my legs my tongue stony
Despair hardening my heavy heart – I came, then,
Into the dead center of that kingdom of death.

                                                  Down there,
It was then – in the blue light fixed in the stone chair frozen,
The chains of a diamond apathy threading the maze of my veins,
Lagered in the mineral corrals of ensorcelling sleep, my eyes
Locked to the bland face of the Queen of the Dead –

                                                      it was then

Then that you came, little Comrade, down the long highways of limestone!
Guiding your ship of light where the dark boats of the dead
Drop down like stone leaves: you came! Through the surf and storm
Of convulsing rock you home to my need: little Son, my Sun!

                *   *   *

Basalt, granite, gabbro, metaphoric marble, contemporary ore –
Era and epoch up to the stony present, the rigid Past
Flows and reshuffles, torn by insurgent winds,
Shocked and reshaped as History changes its sullen face.

And the future groans and turns in its sleep and the past shifts as the New
Is born:
                    Star of blood, with your flag of the underground moon –
That sickle of liberating light – you strike my chains and lead
Me from that throne of death and up the untravelled stairs

Toward the shine of the sun and other stars!
                                        Though one leg be stone
Forever I lag and limp behind you as long as blood
Shall beat in my veins and love shall move as it moves me now,
Chipping the flint of this page to blaze our passage home
Toward the world in the tide of Easter . . .
                                    rising
Into our life as I hear the cries that are resurrecting
There . . .
                    So, we return. We are free in the rhymeless season.
You have struck my foot free from the stone.
                                        Take my hand.
                                            We must not look back.

✦ GUIFFRE'S NIGHTMUSIC

There is moonrise under your fingernail –
Light broken from a black stick
Where your hands in darkness are sorting the probables.

Hunger condenses midnight on the tongue . . .
Journeys . . . Blues . . . ladder of slow bells,
Toward the cold hour of lunar prophecy:

A scale-model city, unlighted, in a shelf
In the knee of the Madonna; a barbwire fence
Strummed by the wind: dream-singing emblems.

– The flags that fly above the breakfast food
   Are not your colors.
                              The republic of the moon
   Gives no sleepy medals. Nor loud ornament.

✦ SOMETIMES

When I take your hand
It is like a door, opening . . .

A garden . . .
A road leading out through a Mediterranean landscape . . .

Finally: a smell of salt,
the port,
A ship leaving for strange and distant countries . . .

✦ RESIDENCIES

So many others have lived in me!
I'm like an old house . . .

Haunted of course –
But many rooms to let!

And the wild garden at the back –
Can you smell?
The honeysuckle the . . .
(Dream compost
                Nightmare Weed)
The moonlight and jasmine . . .

◆ "THE FACE OF THE PRECIPICE IS BLACK WITH LOVERS"

Where are you now –
Little birds of the summer?

Letters still arrive . . .

Through the back window
I see a sparrow
Scatching a living from the snow . . .

♦ NEW POEMS ♦

✦ THE EXCURSION: OR: O COLUMBUS!

This morning is the morning when Mrs. Murphy's treasure chest opens.

All the ladies of the town get out of bed: naked:
Except for their life-preservers – it's a Significant Day!
They put their brassieres on backward.
Then: oilskins. *And*: rubber boots –
Using old garter belts for the proper nautical effect –
And they shinney up their husband's mainmasts to get a brief look
        at the weather,
Singing a stave from Brecht's poem "Ballad of the Pirates":

> "Oh heavenly sky of streaming blue!
> Enormous winds, the sails blow free!
> Let wind and heavens go hang! But oh
> Sweet Mary, let us keep the sea!"

Then just as husband is trying to box the compass, (surprising
Weather, *he's* having) or get a bead on the sun,
The women are off! In marine splendor! They are going Garage
Sailing!

      Sometimes on lakes, sometimes on rivers, sometimes
In ditches, and latecomers surfing on the last of the morning dew!
Tacking and turning seaward to scud the bright blue briny!
A *beautiful* day for garage sailing!
                        And the bay is full
(Or has its fill) of them. And they are so joyful!
Splicing their mizzens and shivering their delicious timbers,
And contriving, by Great Circle lingo, to thwart their neighbor's avasts!

And what garages! Ranch types, terraced with cows and their cowboys;
The Bide-a-wees: vinecovered, their roofs cloudy with Datsuns
Mewing in Japanese against the perilous flood!
There are Swiss chalets, chateaux and simple salt-boxes
Confounding the whelming tide with that good old Puritan jazz,
And the cineramic Protestant rectitude of Increase and Cotton Mather!

Some, captains of gothic garages, are ringing their bells and gargoyles,
While others, late starters, only now, on the meadows of plankton,
Are reviewing their troops (or Old Salts as they may be called),
While the Earlies, Msss. Flotsam and Jetsam, in pelagic disaster areas,
Are seeking the spangled lamp whose dome is deeper and darker
Than any drowned dingle or oceanic boudoir or sea chantey,
Or trying to catch or ketch a bald hornacle on a plate of blue fish,
Or snatch the black pearl of desire from the dens of the iniquitous Deep.

But Mrs. Murphy's treasure chest has long – alas –
Been emptied: by early lovers, couth and uncouth, by kith and kind,
By kindred candid and unkind, by talking heads, heedless
Of her need or nod or now't or naught or nix or nonesuch:
And so the poor woman's bereft – a soul in the dark night
Sailing toward Nowhere among the long black boats of the dead.

Still, here's a drowned dictionary, everything illegible
Except for the words *water* and *salt*. But, as they say,
Who needs it?
    The ladies mount their garages.
          They sail
Back to their homes in Plague Harbor.
         Meanwhile the dictionary
Dries.
   And the word "salvation" appears in the margin!
             Hot

Damn! It's Mrs. Murphy's map to the Enchanted Isles!
But the ladies have gone home again to their own treasures:
Beer cans, children, husbands, mortgages, bills, adultery –
Home Sweet American Home!
       The garages are no longer sailing
And the seas fill up with the sharks of Auld Lang Syne.

✦ THE MIGRATION OF CITIES

We love Paris:
>   The domes of garlic and Gauloises
>   (where the surrealist poets are buried)
>   Rising over the boulevards of hexameters . . .
>   And the Parisian girls, ambassadors of perfume,
>   Sauntering . . . clothed only in moonlight and nostalgia.
>   – Mythic city, capitol of revolutionary longing.

>   The spectral barricades, built from the blood of the Commune,
>   Which remains forever . . . and the red flag of roses and manifestoes
>   Streaming in a wind of bureaucratic sulphur . . .
>   We read the news in the lightning from cemeteries:
>   Starshine reflected from the bones of martyrs.

And we love Florence:
>   Where the cypresses of Fiesole whisper the name of Laura,
>   And the bad-tempered poet: Florentine by birth but not
>   By politics or much of anything else but language
>   Haunts the square where little David takes on the world
>   And all the marble of darkness lies enslumbered in cthonic tombs.

And further:
>   Because the Arno pussyfoots toward the sea
>   Under its clotheslines of bridges hung with the quaint decay
>   Of cages where commerce lived its bright and blighted
>   Infancy and all was for sale: Popes by the yard or the pound.
>   And because Florence is a gate to the cities of the Red north!

And we love Chicago:
>   Though it hog butchers the world –
>   Or as much as New York leaves it. And we love
>   The dense cities of Asia with their auras of inscrutable pain;
>   And of the Mid-East the cities of lace and blood
>   (Each city lifting above itself its former selves:
>   Istanbul, Constantinople, Byzantium

Vaporizing into the irrational Islamic skies
Blue . . .

      dervishes . . .

           Koranic agonies . . .

                  kismet.

And we love the cities of the south with their moonise of gunfire:
Managua . . . heart city . . . horizon of hope –
Madrid of the South "as of this writing" while the world outside my window
Goes by in its idiot clothes, seeking a warmer climate . . .
Tegucigalpa, Guadalajara, Isla Negra
Pah-gotzin-kay, Ciudad Niño Perdido
Salvador Salvador Salvador Salvador Salvador . . .

And I love even little forgotten Pueblo
(In Colorado) for I saw it once: "shining between earth and heaven,"
As the Compañeros and I rode out on a slow freight –
Behind a locomotive powered by tequila and chilis –
Toward nowhere: besotted by wild hope and tortillas.

And still I see the places and the great cities we love
(Landlocked though they may be) sailing out
On the heart-stopping sea toward the Revolutionary Country.
All we need do is cut the anchor chains,
Burn all the contracts and polluted cargo,
Set the captain and owner adrift on a raft,
Shake up the crew and the menu –
And then, the beautiful cities, proudly, under full sail,
Will arrive at the ports which have waited for them so long:
Ports where the Red flag has secretly flown for years.

◆ NUCLEAR WINTER

After the first terror
                    people
Were more helpful to each other –
As in a blizzard
Much comradeliness, help, even
                                        laughter:
The pride of getting through tough times.

Even, months later,
When snow fell in June,
We felt a kind of pride in
                    our
"Unusual weather"
And joked about the wild geese
Migrating south,
Quacking over the 4th of July presidential honkings.
It was, people said,
The way it had been in the Old Days . . .

Until the hunger of the next year.
Then we came to our senses
And began to kill each other.

◆ THE CITIZEN DREAMING

In the blue hour
When the houses fall asleep in their shadows
(Before the impersonal light in the hungry streets
Glamors one more evening)
Then, in one of the mean rooms,
The Citizen makes soup.
On the forbidden hot-plate,
Or, on the forbidden electric fry-pan
(The gift of a grandchild)
Fabricates a sandwich from prefabricated
Processed cheese-type food-type – American type – cheese –
Or opens the innocent-looking can of beans.
The Citizen is dining at home alone in the blue hour.

And now as the darkness distributes crime
Unequally in the streets of the rich and the poor,
The Citizen reviews the day and the days:
The excitements and astonishments of the new age!
The excitement of another rent raise on the room!
The enlightening cut-back in social benefits
By the Presidential thief the Citizen elected!
And the one bar the Citizen could walk to:
closing;
The store that once gave credit:
Gone out of business;
The last movie house the Citizen could get to:
Bankrupt.
And everyone, it seems,
Disappearing:
The children gone impossible distances, the grandchildren
Unknown, unseen . . .

In the blue hour a little light
                         enters.
What was hidden becomes
                         almost

Visible
The opaque
Clears a little
Now that the Citizen has stopped voting for those frauds
(Great heroes once!)
Who have put the Citizen here –
(What was it that a father or mother said?)
Now that it is too late
And the Citizen is as abandoned
As those the Citizen abandoned
Once
Despised
For class or color –
Now all can be seen at last clearly!

Now, in the blue hour the Citizen indulges
In criminal dreams:
A warm place, good food, sex, freedom –
Now that all desires could end only
In the choice of illegal means.

Something human is elected out of the light . . .
In the blue hour.
And the lucky dead on all the roads that led from home to here!

✦ ANNIVERSARIES

for Don and Henrie Gordon

Forty-odd years ago –
Headlines in the snow –
The jobless scrawled a text for mutineers;
Then history seemed sane,
Though Franco sailed for Spain
And Hitler swore to live a thousand years.

Now Progress, his machine,
Makes water out of wine;
With loaves and paper stuffs the multitude;
For power he milks the sun
To see the cities flame
And drives the Goddess from the sacred wood.

Yet anniversaries
Should have our praise, as trees
Salute the queenly coming of the Spring.
All sacred marriages
Keep evergreen in this:
Coupling with Time, they bind him in a ring.

Though time turns, history moves
As if to prove our loves,
Having no pattern but the one we give.
While countries bleed and burn
Not any shall sleep warm
Unless, good friends, you teach us how to live.

Some nine and forty years,
A pulse-beat of the stars,
Astounds the May Fly's million generations.
Your middle style of Time
Is suited most to man.
This whispering wrist sustains the dream of nations.

for Mother Bloor
Mother Jones
Meridel Le Sueur

A tick of time that stones the heads of kings
And drops its pennies on a thousand eyes
Unreels the gaudy shroud of history
And transmutes all statistics into pain.

What is simple virtue can never be denied,
Explained, or cancelled. Still, it is not
Enough to love a world that must be changed.
This was the earliest thing they learned.

Neither Weehawken Ferry nor a flower,
The world was love and work – we could become
Human. Across the cruel geography
Of strike and struggle, hitch-hiking, riding freights

They sought the boundaries of that possible world
Where statistical death can never cancel dream
And history is humanized. Their blazoning voyage
Points toward the Indies of our mortal wish.

♦ THE BLACK TRAIN

I'm still struck (as when I saw my first Pasque-flower)
Now, at a single soft shoot of daffodil arching, slow,
Through the face of the rock-like ground and on: up: through
The flinty shingle of March-blown sleet and snow
On the winter-wasted ice-bound lawns of Milwaukee Avenue.

Spring was a million adjectives: once: one noun:
All green and milky: furry as pussy-willow . . . sweet . . .
As the blood of maple. But the gleamy stealth of gold in the
                    river-winding wood
Blurs quicksand or flood. And spider-silk blinds and binds.
Then mullein, purslane, milfoil, milkweed, dandelions . . . tiresome.

Summer wearies me . . . Endless the combers of wheat: gold:
Endless in amber distance. And the endless dance of the aspenleaf
Tires. No new word in the mile-long rasp and rattle: endless
Corn-gossip. The grasshopper burdens and the humblebee is no friend.
But I'm glad the homeless sleep warm in this landlords' season.

Autumn tires and conspires: draws forth its druggy water
Where the dreamy souls of strolling poets drown, slow,
In their little ecstasies. Troll fire seams the north woods:
Ghosts of goatsbeard false bird's nests of Queen Anne's lace
Tourists divining with goldenrod beside sluggish rivers . . .

Stern winter frowns. A stiffening mortal rigor
Sets flowerheads rolling and the crowns of summer fall.
Moral as death, a white stealth, cold, beards all the grass
That robes, on sunny thrones in its last and desperate green: false.
False-foxy all: the green of autumn and the gold of spring.

I've lived inland too long. It sickens me –
Land islanded. Winter may harden. But spring unties
All icy strings. Fools'-gold of summer. Treacherous trollopy autumn . . .
No. Enough of this comic death-dance. I long, in mortal longing,
For the shine and silence, the flash and wallop of the sea.

Somewhere in that sea, still, on a tide-bound salt siding,
Hunched, a black train halts, sighing and clanking, slouched, crafty,
Breathing like a rusty pump and waiting for bills of lading.
The telegraph office clicks its beads and abacus, ticks and chatters,
And the empty cars wait for the black train to head inland.

✦ PRAISES IV

On the Beauty and the Wonders of Women
And Some of the Problems Attendant Thereunto

I wake in the early dawn and my hand has fallen asleep,
(Bedded between her legs in the nest of her sex)
And is dreaming it is a bird – my left and dreaming hand.
And the birds begin: footnoting the long paragraphs of the light
That are daybreak – birds she will scold for presumption when she awakes.
I move my hand. She whimpers. But her own dream still holds.
I drag this dream-hand into my life . . .

                                    Suddenly Spring
Fills all the house, the county –
                          maybe the whole world –
With the odor of orchards, gardens, orange blossoms, attars,
Essences: musk, civet, ambergris, frangipani,
Emanations, effluvia, eidolons – volatile oils sweeter
Than all the perfumes of Araby assault my sense and my soul!

My god, I must be Huysmans! – I think I've invented his scent
Organ – or at least harmonium. Next thing I know I'll be writing
Au Rebours, sparking the Goncourts or Remy Gourmand or Gourmet!
And it's Guermantes all the way in this swan-like or Proustian light.

But it's *not* that. It's just ("just" think of it! – "just" !) –
My hand which has come from between her legs where her cunt and my spunk
In the dialectic of essences formed this sacred fragrance
All else sublimed away . . .
                        And now it's loose in the world!
Like the hand of a prophet!

                      And what will the neighbors say?
                                    Oh, I hear them
Groan and laugh in their sleep and the street has both ends flapping
Like an oversized wig on a windy day as a most un-Lutheran lust
Is loosed in the glacial bedrooms of the sensible petty bourgeois!
They'll be coming to get us, girl! How can you sleep and slumber?
Fuck off, care-charmer sleep, thou son of the sable night!

But that's an alarmist thought – time now for Irish cunning . . .
What can I do to save this taboo hieratic hand?
It can't, in the back garden, like a dog's bone be buried,
And it's not the kind of a thing you can take to your local bank –
Considering the box it came from no safety deposit system
Will hold this myrrh and frankincense – the Three Wisemen
Would arrive early this year and stick up the dismal joint!
And all the investors would come, and anyone with a loose dime
Would start an account – and they'd all, by god, *live* there
Eating from the giveaway pots and pans burning the tellers for fuel!

What a scandal! Copulating among mortgages
And second mortgages: everyone: getting off on the scent.
And they'll call in the Federal Reserve and the National Guard and Oh god! –
Annuit Coeptis . . .
                    End of the world as we know it.
                                        And all for a hand!
Perhaps a secret account in Switzerland. . . .
                                        But then the dollar
Would fall and the whole slave world would have to live on the yen
This hand produces without even lifting a finger.

It is not an easy problem to solve – what to do with this hand.
It has never been faced before by another living man . . .
Perhaps by sleight-of-hand I can charm it away?
                                        Or demount it?
Then, like a pressed flower, I could fold it up in a book.
Little five-leaf clover from the world's ten fateful fields,
Spade-handed ugly peasant appendage that she has made perfect . . .

Excellent! Excellent . . . But what book will I choose?
Marx's *Capital* comes to mind . . . safe from the liberals
And all econ professors – but what of the Thought Police?
Their sacred quest for the Word . . . anything underlined?
So maybe the bible – one of the lagered and barbwire books

All *don'ts* and *do's*, the Angel in irons, Mr. Moses Moreso.
But this hand would confound all law: theologic, economic and bourgeois.
And just as I insert it (where meat is forbidden) it jumps
Into Apocalypse! Turns to a burning bush and sends
Bluebirds of purest flame to aid the World Revolution!

Envoi

Comrades, if we had more of these hands we *could* make love, not war.
And neighbors: more of these shennhandigans could change the world
without arms!

✦ REDISCOVERY

Once more I go over your earthly body:
Come out of the tent of your hair, surprised by the strength of your neck –
That road of ivory and moonlight.
Acropolis of your brow – I look for the Persian ponies!
And then your eyes: close-up – out of focus like mine –
These haunted lakes where I see myself rising from another life:
My life on the tenth continent where I count stones for a living . . .
None of them shining with the blue of passports.
Your mouth is soft as your cunt and invites me in,
But I go my journey as I have before and will again . . .

Shoulders under the cloud of your hair like sacred mountains
My tribe has always worshipped . . .

                                        and then the hills of your breasts –
Which are neither big nor little: the merest perfection:
Each one the size of my hand and the weight of my heart!
The little owls that house at the points of those breasts
Are wakeful now – the lookouts are alert and rise to meet me.
They offer me tincture of bread and a little salt –
As they stand, each in her ring – the little birds of your breasts
Which I take in my mouth as you take mine in yours.

A hint of civet there, as if wild things had crossed a meadow
Just after a light rain . . .

                                and deep in your breasts I hear
The secret fountains, water of life, the milk my body
Aches to set flowing – "honey of generation" Yeats
Said.
            Then: the open flower of your mouth and the white bees
Of your teeth that gather my honey from parishes far and near.
Throughout my now-blossoming flesh and into the hive of my cock . . .

Ah, but you are a long woman, my Slim, my Silky.
I can never travel you all – not in one night – or a life –
But I go my impossible pilgrimage, my holy voyage,
Enjoying the landscapes. My eyes, open or closed –
I know every highlight of this golden road and every halt and historic

Landmark we put there!
                    It is slow travel,
                                        by tongue.
I am fed and famished in this burning snow!
Not even love is enough! I send out my soul-cock:
With our bodies ablaze we are fucking on all the astral planes!

And by that light I go on burning, fainting and burning –
At my priestly labors: blessing the coves and coasts of your body.
O, my Again-Found Land: like a friar of Magellan I rove
Over and inward on this fiery plain: breathing, alive,
In atmospheres others would die in – my own and yours – eating
Only the celestial salt sublimed from our mutual sweat.
And now I have come to our Southern Cross, where the hairs on your belly,
Golden, glint a lighter gold than the gold sheen of your flesh!
Here all directions change and new constellations are born!

Vain efforts . . .
The lovers' groan and pant, frantic to get beyond
Body.
          And spirit laughs or shivers
                                        trembling
                                                  like a virgin bride:
Waiting a marriage of heaven and hell in the bed of this world.

✦ BEHOLD THE WOMAN

1.

This shawl of hair and sighs
This long legged complaint
This vessel of hope and hunger going forth on a cold morning
This grave as long as a lifetime
This endless ardor
This waterproof package of desire wet by internal tears
This constant confabulation of icons and landscapes:
You: barefaced plan for the five eternities
The eternity of
                    Fire
                         Water
                              Earth
                                   Air
                                        and the fifth element
You, comic extension of spirit
Under the tragic mask.

2.

Because body is tragic while spirit can step free.
Because body is hunger leading toward death.
Body suffers for spirit to create more spirit.
And defies spirit so that spirit may wither or grow.
Body would deny death to the amusement of spirit.
Body would deny death to put love in place of spirit.
Body would deny death to the consternation of all process.
Body would annul time and because it would annul time body is trapped
            in time.
Desire moves body – so all must be paid for in time . . .

3.

But body can transcend time through desire and dream.
And dream can transform desire when desire goes beyond body.
And desire becomes dream again when it goes beyond itself.
Ah, woman! – cinched and sinued to the immanent world
By your pubic hair . . .
                    O vessel of earthly longing,
Carrier of what is most sane in the general dream . . .
As you sail out into the unknown sea,
A child goes forth under the changed constellations.

◆ OFFERING

Father, you must have been,
Like now –
On a tiny raft while the big ship went down.

You had taken our mother aboard
While the decks were still awash.
Then, for a little time, it must have seemed almost like heaven –
Though you've never said that
In words.
Nor has she
         but I saw it
In both your eyes when you thought
We were not watching.

Heaven, then.
Even on the dark and shoreless waters.
Other rafts went down. Around you cries
Went up –
         agonies –
Sharks clouding and clotting in the sea –
Heaven.

Then our mother began
Presenting us to you:
One, every couple of years,
Was conjured out of the gypsy tent of her black skirts.
And you fed us:
Fishing all night in the hungry waters,
Giving your clothing to warm us,
And you naked, shivering in the cold,
                 enduring –
Why didn't you drown us like a litter of sick cats?

But . . . didn't.
You gave your freedom for our mother's fulfillment.
And you gave us
All the lost honey of a young man's years –
Steering through the vicious seas of those bitter times . . .
Ah . . . dearest father, dear
Helmsman!

◆ THE USE OF BOOKS

What's there to praise.
In that vast library of long gone days
Bound in the failed and fading leather
Of ancient weather?

To free what's trapped or bound
Is my whole law and ground:
Since it's myself I find
Out on the rough roads travelling blind.

Yet, for another's use,
I bind what I let loose
So others may make free
Of those lost finds no longer use to me.

✦ WAR RESISTERS' SONG

Come live with me and be my love
And we will all the pleasures prove –
Or such as presidents may spare
Within the decorum of Total War.

By bosky glades, by babbling streams
(Babbling of Fission, His remains)
We discover happiness' isotope
And live the half-life of our hope.

While Geiger counters sweetly click
In concentration camps we'll fuck.
Called traitors? That's but sticks and stones
We've Strontium 90 in our bones!

And thus, adjusted to our lot,
Our kisses will be doubly hot –
Fornicating (like good machines)
We'll try the chances of our genes.

So (if Insufficient Grace
Hath not fouled thy secret place
Nor fall-out burnt my balls away)
Who knows? but we may get a boy –

Some paragon with but one head
And no more brains than is allowed;
And between his legs, where once was love,
Monsters to pack the future with.

✦ PEOPLE ARE SO BUSY: OR: THAT'S LIFE!

The dying man
Lifts his head.
Someone wants
To borrow his bed.

✦ THE INHERITANCE

Like well diggers
The woodpeckers tunnel.
The spring mornings . . .
Green stopes and galleries
Where, later, the little owls
Will drink the darkness.

✦ ONCE WE MEANT IT

"We'll meet in Madrid
In thirty-six!"
But Fascist Franco
Carried the day.

"In gay Paree
In forty-three!"
It took a war
To keep us away.

"We'll see you soon,
Since you've come home."
We say it now
For something to say.

✦ THE NEED FOR STOICISM
IN THE STOA OF ATTALUS

The pitcher that went to the well too often
Has a mighty crack,
And the balls on some of the statues are sadly shot,
The GE drinking fountain is out of whack,
And the urinals (by Crane) have all gone to pot.

✦ THE EDGE OF THE RIVER

It has been a long journey.
And now, at the end of it,
Like a boat that broke free and drifted far down the river,
I come to rest on an unknown shore:
Half in, half out
Of the water.

◆ COLUMBUS

Columbus, wearing a night-gown made from a treasure map,
Is sleepwalking on the giant avenues of an invisible sea.

He dreams he had discovered the Isthmus of Compound Interest
In his constant pursuit of the droppings of the One Historical Zero.
Tears fall through the meridians of his hands.
He is sad. His sadness makes the winds blow,

Filling his sails with the algebra of abstract labor.
Birds faint at his passing and the fish turn to stone.
He is looking for gold that breathes and has dark skin
And can be renamed *Slave*. The birds revive, screaming.

In the dungeons of the King the dark zero grows wounds and weapons.
At sea the waves trudge off in search of a new continent.

◆ PORTENTS

Today they invent
The computer that invents
Computers.

Tomorrow – who knows? –
The wheel.
After that,
Sooner or later,
Fire.

◆ THE UNDERGROUND

I.

Cities arise . . .
Like bric-a-brac on mountains which have not yet been named.
Here, the Pioneers
Arrived, drugged and armed to the eyes, on high-flying bombers –
And most of them think they are still in the flat lands to the west.
Here, on the good days,
In those serious, born-again, apparently-sufficient, imperialist climes –
Where all days are apparently good days the cities ornament themselves:
Among the desolate monsters that sometimes appear after midnight
(Escaped from below) statues spring into being: presidents,
Generals at the center of circles and squares – stars where converging
Streets may be commanded by gunfire . . .
                                  L'Etoile est plus belle, n'est-ce pas?
Oui. Beautiful.
                Et le mitrailleuse de ma tante, aussi.
But my aunt's machine-gun does not command all vistas, for –

Meanwhile, below,
In stopes black as the bore of an outlaw Frontier Colt
(And among the mnemonic plagues of heuristic condemned numbers)
The miners are tearing gold out of the rocks
With their bare hands.
                        Down here all the machines have failed:
The machines with spark-plugs fired by patriotic cliches
And burning the blood of children in cylinders of law and homicide . . .

Aloft, from balconies spun from hallucinatory silk,
The ladies climb the vertiginous ladders of afternoon TV sex.
(Those same ladders which have only one end).
Their eyes, brilliant with boredom, gaze down the grand avenues
Toward Presidential palaces with their glowing facades of caviar.
The weather is petrified in its windless theater of ice,
And the seasons have been vanished and replaced by appropriate music.
Moon of hypocrites . . .
                        light . . .
                                stiffened by black glass . . .
Tomorrow: high tea in the execution chamber.

II.

Underground, the weather goes on in the dim streets:
Among marooned motorcycles dead of too much salvation.
(Mourned by the little cadenzas of torn-out tongues.)
Here are the immense catalogs of lost meat:
The broken wrists of black-gowned washerwomen
The blind tearing off the skin of their eyes to see
The starving child who has eaten his own arm to the elbow
The old who sit in the plaza with guitars full of plastic explosive
And unwanted sex –
                           here the miners return from their last
Shot in the dark.
                     Now the square is filled.
                                    They await the *Indios* . . .

III.

In the bat-freaking twilight, *crepuscule du soir*,
And down along the old soignée river, the rich
Salauds and assholes, on elite terraces, suffering, perhaps,
From imperfect coronary recall or the rancours of the memory, see,
The necrotic marble of those clouds which are now being towed
Into the blood-warm skies of saltpetre and semen . . .

Yes, lovely twilight up there: the ladies, in electronic nightgowns
Watch while a stone cutter, snatched by night from below,
Is chiselling in granite, over the graveyard entrance:
NO IDEAS BUT IN THINGS
                     And right behind him, another,
(Free-lance) AND NO THINGS WITHOUT SOME GODDAMN KIND
OF IDEA *ABOUT* THEM!

IV.

                               Below in the underground square, the peasants,
Drawn by the silver bells of their tiny burros arrive
From the Capitalist and Cocaine dictatorships of imperialist duchies,
Colonies of the dollar and longtime fiefdoms of the CIA.
Now, in the little fiesta of the damned, songs are exchanged,
And tentative sex, and stories are told and politics
Made clear.
                The guns are given.
                            The day of the Rising is set.

V.

Meanwhile, above, in the city,
The elite take to their arms the Commodity Fetish: in boudoirs
Where (the moonlight clotting those mythologies of power and drugs)
The glaciers have set up their tents.

✦ NEAR PAH-GOTZIN-KAY

I.

BABES IN THE WOODS

Dry birch logs:
Blue flame and incense.
Everything we need to say written in smoke
Now on these burning sheets.

Understand how we got here:
Parachuted in from a disastrous sector
Of the contemporary war.
Lost our clothes in the freezing cold – she did, so I threw mine away –
And here we are in front of the fire in the cabin.
Wood enough for the week.
Moon in Scorpio over the frozen lake
And the wolves singing around us,
Nothing to read but *Sonnets from the Portuguese.*

Seems simple; but wait till the neighbors come over.
They want to play whist – and that's hard: holding all those cards
In our hands and teeth
And trying to bid while the other hand holds our blanket
(And whose hand is *that*?) to cover what they call our nakedness –
Something that seems to us like our own selves –
Something, in the long nights,
We wrap ourselves in.

This game can go on a long time.
Looks like we'll never win.

II.

GOING FOR WATER

In the morning the snow is deeper
And the river is sleeping a cold sleep.
"Come back in summer," Water says, from somewhere in bed;
"I'm going to sleep with Miss Rock the rest of the winter."

✦ BEYOND SEATTLE

Far islands . . . veiled by cold rain.
Beaches lighted by a million candle-fish.
Snow on the mountain.
Salmon at the mouth of the river.

✦ DEPRIVATION

The dull knife cuts our hand –
It has felt neglected,
Thirsty,
For a long time.

✦ IN DREAM TIME

Dear Tomasito:
We talk about dreams.
Yours always amaze me,
Though you've moved out
Beyond the castles.

As for me
I seem to spend many nights
Walking a perimeter of rotten ice
Around a bad break
Where someone less lucky
Just had a last fall.

✦ IN SICKNESS LIKE SLEEP

It is like this perhaps
That the great tree of darkness
(Of which we have seen only a few leaves –
Or, perhaps a few, its black flower)
Will gather us into its shade.

◆ FLINT AND STEEL

Mountain
  Mesquite
    Sea
      Star
        Flower
          – All the imperial nouns
    In their presumed autonomy
    Waiting
    For the little verb that will kindle the fire!

◆ THE FATIGUE OF OBJECTS

In the victim's room,
The dust grows bored,
Waiting, on the knife handle,
For the fingerprints of the murderer.

◆ LONG GOODBYE

A few leaves remain.
But the old cottonwood
No longer remembers them.

✦ MEDITERRANEAN

1.

I passed you many times as I went down the cliff walk,
Little Olivetree, all stunted and stiffened, as you climbed
From the blue cove where the cold sea comes in and dies.

I never saw you. My eyes were fixed: stunned
By the brutal light dancing in the fields of the insane blue.
The entrancing sea – indeed! I crowhopped and balked at seeing –

At seeing you, Comrade Olive. I had too much seaing.
And what were you pointing to or away from – your arthritic hands
Pinned in their tattered gray-green gloves, the fineries of former days?

2.

But finally I had to see you: old, fruitless, lame.
Were you climbing toward fire to bake the bread of the drowned
                    fisherman's widow?
Or be crosscut to bed the village lovers fucking themselves insane

And back again while peasants, donkeys, women and kids
Listening applauded, sniggered or looked unappeasably sad?
Was it for this you shook all night in the cold salt fogs of the sea?

I don't understand you – thanks be to all gods, goddesses and godlets!
You are not human – and thanks be again for *that*!
You are just *there* – unnoticed except for scent-posting dogs

Who piss on your gnarly roots each morning and twice on Sunday.
Relentless as the sea that rages daily in the shattered light –
Old guerilla: charging slow motion to take high ground!

You seem to want to be helpful to those up there in the village . . .
Ergo my fancy of fire – your sacrificial death.
Such fancies can breed theologies; baroque and green as pond-scum.

3.

Nothing like bad Greek beer to clear the weary mind!
It seems, Comrade Olive, that you have got where we all
Will get. And I salute you, old fellow-traveler!

I halt, take a spray of your leaves and stride to a bar at the cove.
The sky is blessing the sea and the sea is blessing the sky!
Ho hum. Sycophants. Mutually co-admiring. But the beer is cold.

And I love this spray of olive leaves: gray and crazing
With frosty filigree of salt. I suck them. And the beer tastes fine.
So there is a grace from the halt by the tree; though not amazing.
May be: best thing: endure: face front: get back on the line.

✦ SELECTED BIBLIOGRAPHY

First Manifesto, Alan Swallow: Baton Rouge, 1940. (Swallow Pamphlet No. 1)

Three Young Poets, selected by Alan Swallow, The Press of J. A. Decker; Prairie City, Illinois, 1942.

To Walk a Crooked Mile, Alan Swallow: New York, 1947.

Longshot O'Leary's Garland of Practical Poesie, International Publishers: New York, 1949.

Witness to the Times! privately printed, 1954.

Figures from a Double World, Alan Swallow: Denver, 1955 (Swallow poetry book award of 1954).

The Gates of Ivory, The Gates of Horn, with a foreword by Charles Humboldt, Mainstream Publishers: New York, 1957. (Novel)

About Clouds, illustrated by Chris Jenkyns, Melmont Publishers: Los Angeles, 1959. (Children's book)

Letter to an Imaginary Friend, Part I, Alan Swallow: Denver, 1962.

New and Selected Poems, Alan Swallow: Denver, 1962.

Letter to an Imaginary Friend, Parts I and II, Swallow Press: Chicago, 1970.

The Movie at the End of the World: Collected Poems, Swallow Press: Chicago, 1973. Paper ed. 1980, U. of Ohio Press.

A Sound of One Hand, Minnesota Writers Publishing House, 1975.

Voices from Beyond the Wall, Territorial Press, Moorhead, 1974.

Open Songs, Uzzano Press, Mr. Carroll, 1977.

Letter to Tomasito, Holy Cow! Press, Minneapolis, 1977.

Trinc: Praises II, Copper Canyon Press, 1979.

Waiting for the Angel, Uzzano Press, 1979.

Passages Toward the Dark, Copper Canyon Press, 1982.

Echoes Inside the Labyrinth, Thunder's Mouth Press, 1983.

Letter to an Imaginary Friend, Parts III and IV, Copper Canyon Press, 1985.

The Gates of Ivory, The Gates of Horn, republished, Another Chicago Press, 1987.

Thomas McGrath was born on a North Dakota farm in 1916. He was educated at the University of North Dakota, Louisiana State University, and New College, Oxford University, where he was a Rhodes Scholar. He served in the Air Force in the Aleutians during World War II. He has taught at colleges and universities in Maine, California, New York, North Dakota, and Minnesota. Between periods of teaching, he was a free lance writer of fiction and film, particularly documentary film. He held the Amy Lowell Travelling Poetry Scholarship for 1965–66, received a Guggenheim Fellowship in 1968, Bush Foundation Fellowships in 1976 and 1981. In 1987, he was awarded a Senior Fellowship by the Literature Program of the National Endowment for the Arts.

The types in this book are Aldus and Palatino,
designed by Hermann Zapf.
Composition by Fjord Press Typography.
Book design by Tree Swenson.
Manufactured by McNaughton & Gunn.